Baba's Rinanubandh

Leelas during His Sojourn in Shirdi

Baba's Rinanubandh

Leelas during His Sojourn in Shirdi

Vinny Chitluri

Sterling Paperbacks

STERLING PAPERBACKS
An imprint of
Sterling Publishers (P) Ltd.
A-59, Okhla Industrial Area, Phase-II,
New Delhi-110020.
Tel: 26387070, 26386209; Fax: 91-11-26383788
E-mail: sterlingpublishers@airtelbroadband.in
ghai@nde.vsnl.net.in
www.sterlingpublishers.com

Baba's Rinanubandh
© 2007, Vinny Chitluri
ISBN 978-81-207-3403-6
Reprint 2008

Printed and Published by Sterling Publishers Pvt. Ltd.,
New Delhi-110020.

Preface

My father in 1950, on one of his visits to Shirdi brought
N.V. Gunaji's *Shri Sai Satcharita*. We took turns to read
it. At that time I read it more like a storybook. I learned about
Baba's leelas and His divinity. Through the years I read and
reread it. But I could not understand many things. For
instance, Mrs Tarkhad's son was sitting in the Dwarkamai
right in front of Baba, yet he wanted to return home to offer
naivedya to the photograph? Who was this child? Why
couldn't he just offer naivedya to the Shaktar Ishwar sitting in
front of him? Was there another story in this story? (*Shri Sai
Satcharita*, Chapter 9].

It bothered me a lot that Baba who had control of the
elements [*Shri Sai Satcharita*, Chapter 11] who was "Deva di
Dev" [God of God's] lost a wrestling bout with Mohiddin?
[Chapter 5]. The Parabhrama, who made this *shrishti*
[cosmos], and guided it! He who was omnipresent and
omnipotent, after losing this match wore a torn *kafni*. Why a
Kafni? What did it symbolise? Baba, though God Almighty on
a personal level was close to the common man, the rustic
villager; the well educated, and famous devotee. The rich and
the poor, the famous and not so famous flocked to His feet.
Was it because of His 'chamatkars'? Or was it His equality of
vision? Was there something deeper, a *rinanubandh* [karmic
ties or debt] that brought them to Shirdi? They came not
knowing what to expect! And they stayed devoted to Baba for
the rest of their lives. His divinity, His love, and compassion,
His equality of vision endeared Him to every devotee.

Almost in each and every chapter of the *Shri Sai Satcharita* there are portions, words and parables that I could not understand. So I set out trying to find some answers. Along the way I met the descendants of these "Ankita Bhaktas". I pestered them with questions about their grandparents. I read various books, old *Sai Leela* magazines, and other books and found some answers there. At other times I drove my friend Manjula nuts. I coerced her to read the *Upanishads* and *Nirukti* and find answers for me. "Do anything, read anything but give me answers with references," I said. And she did. That's what Gurus are supposed to do! Not all the material is in this book. I for one found many answers. As I am sure many of you did. Some I have included, and you may have found other answers. But at least it is a start.

This book is a kaleidoscope, of leelas, photographs, and lives of some devotees which illustrate the karmic and rinanubandhic ties with Baba. I strongly believe that the visuals stay with us for a long time. I hope, that this book will make reading of *Shri Sai Satcharita* easier and fruitful.

Vinny Chitluri

Acknowledgements

I owe a debt of gratitude to Sada S Ghode for searching for the descendants of these devotees. Gladly he set out armed with "No names except those mentioned in the *Shri Sai Satcharita*. No addresses. No telephone numbers. Except a great deal of faith in Baba". Often he would ask strangers if they knew this devotee, and the stranger would say, "These days its hard to find someone with a complete address and phone number. And you are asking for a name, which is at least eighty-years-old. Good luck". But Sada felt deeply that with Baba's work nothing is impossible. And he did find them. "How?" I would ask. "Through Baba", he would say calmly.

I am also grateful to my friend and mentor Manjula S from Bangalore, who searched for the answers. She would patiently explain again and again the meaning of the Sanskrit words. Frantically I would call her day and night asking if she had done the homework, I had given her, especially on Siddique Phalke. "Baba uses the number twelve a lot. What could it mean?" I would say. Manjula would send me books on numerology and various other materials. That was not available to me. Then she would explain it till I was satisfied. Thank you my dear friend.

I am thankful to V.V Leeladhar from Hyderabad, who made innumerable trips to Shirdi to scan the photographs and do all that was involved with the computer, as I am quite computer illiterate. He happily helped me in so many ways that it's impossible to mention.

I would also like to thank Mr Surinder Ghai and his staff who spent a great deal of time with me, helping me in innumerable ways and publishing this book.

Last but not the least, I thank each and every Baba bhakta who opened their homes and their hearts to Sada. Allowing him to take photographs and telling him everything that they knew about their ancestors. They answered his questions with infinite patience and grace.

Vinny Chitluri

Contents

**Dev Baba alias
Anant Prabhu Walavalkar**

Rajaram Kaka (Dev Baba's father) hailed from Walaval, Sindhudurga Jilha (region). Hence, they were called the 'Walavalkars'. His lineage was from the Sathkul Kudar Deshkar family. The family was very devout and religious. He married Krishnabai alias Sitabai who was Dabholkar's daughter, in 1916.

The couple moved to Girgaum, Bombay, where Rajaram worked in the Accountant General's Office. He was devoted to Vitthal and followed the Warkari Sampradaya [A sect of devotees who walk to a holy place or temple, usually to Pandarpur]. Dev Baba (photo 10) was the eldest of the four brothers and one sister. As Girgaum was rather a remote suburb, Rajaram, and his family moved to Dadar. As it was the first pregnancy, Sitabai came to her parents' home in Bandra. Sitabai was rather ill during the pregnancy and had *nandavayu* (possibly tetanus).

Dabholkar was very concerned. So, he ran to Shirdi and told Baba about it. Baba reassured him and said, "Balantpan nirvigna hoyeel" [The delivery will be trouble free]. He also stated that His son would be born to her. Assured by Baba's words, Dabholkar returned home and prayed to Baba for help. Rajaram also prayed earnestly to Vitthal, begging Him to give him a Dnyaneshwar like son. The time for delivery arrived and Dabholkar anxiously waited outside.

It was 13th April, 1918, when he finally went to see his daughter and was surprised at what he saw. The mother had thrown the child in a corner, and would not touch or cuddle him. The child however lay contentedly in the corner. But what surprised him most was the halo of light around his head. He also had an aura of light around him.

As the mother was afraid to hold her child, she also refused to nurse him. Dabholkar however picked up the child and brought him to Shirdi. He went straight to Dwarkamai and laid him at Baba's feet. Being rather anxious and distraught at his daughter's behaviour, he told Baba all that had happened in great detail. Meanwhile, Baba picked up the baby, and laying him in His lap, patted him gently. Then, He nursed him by placing His thumb in the child's mouth. The baby sucked and out came the milk.

In the *Shri Sai Satcharita* (Chapter 4), the beautiful Leela of Baba is given where Baba tells Das Ganu (photo 79) that he need not go to Prayag to have a bath in the Ganga and Jamuna. When Das Ganu lays his head on Baba's feet, out flows the Ganga and Jamûna from Baba's toes. Here, Baba feeds the tiny baby from His thumb. The Sanskrit word for thumb is *angusta*. Baal Krishna [infant Krishna] is usually seen with His thumb in His mouth, as milk would come out. Here Baba nurses Dev Baba with His thumb.

In the *Probodha Sudhakara* written by Sri Sankaracharya there is a beautiful verse, the meaning of it is given below.

The celestial Ganga is considered as emanating from the feet of Vishnu [regarded as Krishna] and, when it was brought to earth, Shiva is stated to have borne it on his head to reduce its force. The idea conveyed in this verse is that Krishna is Sat Chit Anand. And is the soul and basis of all universes, gods, and beings. So Baba is none other than Vishnu or Krishna.

Dev Baba had Baba's grace around him at all times. His primary education was in Marathi medium. Then he went to Wilson English Medium School. However, Dev Baba rarely attended school. He spent most of his time meditating at the Swami Samarth Math nearby. Swami Samarth also blessed him. As a young man, he joined the Kurla Municipal Kirde Kendra as a teacher in physical education. He was extremely fond of his students and was fair to each and everyone. However, the students were from two castes, and one caste felt that Dev Baba was 'rather fond and sympathetic to the other caste'. They went and complained to the other teachers. One of the teachers decided to give him a good thrashing. Meanwhile, some of the teachers informed Dev Baba of the plan. Casually, he said, "Oh, but he will not come to school tomorrow." And so, it came to pass that the teacher went to swim that evening, drowned and died. When this happened, Dev Baba realised that Baba had bestowed him with *siddhis*.

He decided not to work for anybody, but to utilise his services for God. He made various pilgrimages and stayed in the Himalayas. He learned Hata Yoga and progressed spiritually.

In 1945, Dev Baba's mother was seriously ill and he knew that she would soon pass away. He visited her and gave her a mantra to recite. Then he came to Shirdi and sat in the Samadhi Mandir and did *parayana* [reading a holy book or *pothi* in a set number of days, usually seven days] of the *Shri Sai Satcharita*. While he was mid-way, he received a telegram, saying that his mother had taken a turn for the worse. He asked Baba whether he should go and visit her. Baba said, 'Yes'. Now, he was in a quandary as to how he would go that far in such a short time. He was pondering as to why Baba had granted him permission when the time was so short and the journey, so long.

Lo! Baba stood before him and reassured him. Baba had brought a horse and asked him to accompany Him in the *shooksbma* (invisible) form. They both reached Dadar. He met his mother and gently reassured her of a peaceful death and that Baba Himself was there to take care of her destination. Thus, it came to pass that she died peacefully. He returned to Shirdi and completed the parayana. When he told people about his mother's death, they looked at him with astonishment and did not believe him, 'as he was seated for parayana all that time'.

In 1952, he married Kishori Bai who shared his devotion for Baba and worked along with him. The couple moved to Ambarnath and stayed in their ancestral home. On the first floor, a *mandir* was made in 1967. A *saat-dhaatu murti* (an idol of seven metals) was installed and *pratishtha* performed.

Dev Baba had many followers and he guided them to his Ishtadev Sai Baba. After a very fruitful life, he took samadhi on Thursday, May 25th, 1994 on Vaishakh Vaidya Apara Ekadashi. He asked his relatives not to perform any rituals or religious ceremonies.

(Ref: *Dev Babanche Charita (Marathi)*, 26th May, 1996)

Leela 2: **Anandrao Trimbak Karnik**

This 'big sparrow' was pulled by Baba in 1911. Nana Chandorkar and Ram Maruti (mentioned in Khaparde's *Shirdi Diary*, page 26) were instrumental for Anandrao Trimbak Karnik's visit to Shirdi. Karnik knew Ram Maruti for quite a long time. And the Chandorkar's were family friends and neighbours at Kalyan. Indeed, Karnik and Nana went to the same school and were childhood friends. Later, Nana moved away to pursue higher studies and to search for employment.

In 1911, Nana went to Karnik's home to renew their old friendship. As always, Nana spoke of Baba, narrating His leelas in great detail and describing His divinity. Thus, the first seed of faith was sowed. Nana Chandorkar also had Das Ganu to perform *bhajans* at his residence. Ram Maruti usually attended the bhajan programmes and danced and jumped in bliss.

Karnik and his sons started attending the *bhajans*. At the end of 1911, Karnik had completed his fasts for *pradosh*

(Udyapan). It also happened to be an evening of the bhajan. He eagerly went to Nana's home. There he met Ram Maruti and asked him if he could give him *Anugraha* and *Mantra updesh*. Unhesitatingly, Ram Maruti pointed to Baba's photograph and asked him to seek refuge at Baba's feet. A few days earlier, his eldest son expressed his desire to go to Shirdi. So, taking Ram Maruti's advice, they took off to Shirdi.

Before leaving Kalyan, he had mentally decided upon two things. First to offer Baba *sava rupya* (one and a quarter rupees) as *dakshina*, as he firmly believed that it was the dakshina of Shri Satya Narayana's Mahapuja. And secondly that if the Baba of His own accord did not ask for dakshina, he would return home.

After a comfortable journey, they alighted at Kopargaon. There, they met Ram Maruti with a whole lot of his disciples setting off to Shirdi. The group of disciples hired the only bullock cart that was available and proceeded to Shirdi. Karnik and his son were thus stranded, or so they thought. However, both had mentally decided to go to Shirdi, come what may. A short while later, a *tonga* turned up and offered to take them to Shirdi.

The journey was very comfortable and on reaching Shirdi, the *tonga walla* [driver] asked karnik for a very fair fare. He gladly gave it and went to the Dwarkamai. He took *darshan*, and attended the *aarati* with great joy. Baba however called his son to Him and asked him for dakshina and *prasad*. His wife had prepared this *prasad* with great love and devotion, hoping that Baba would accept it. Karnik did *charanseva*, but Baba did not even glance at him, or so it seemed. He gave his son *aashirwad* and applied *udi* repeatedly on his forehead. Then, Baba ordered everyone to go to the Wada and sit there peacefully. Karnik was in a dilemma, as Baba had not asked for dakshina; so was he to return home? Then Baba looked directly at him and said, "Do not leave Shirdi without my permission. Now, go to the Wada."

Now, Karnik was in a real dilemma. He had to return home as his son had to attend office the next day. So a little later, Karnik and his son went to meet Baba, but He wasn't there. On the third attempt, Baba was there. However, he called his son into the Sanctum Sanctorum and asked Karnik to wait in the Sabha Mandap. "Bhokrutva konas chuktas naahi, te bhogtlech pahije" [Suffering does not allude anyone and it has to be borne]. His son was in a very weakened state, following a long illness at that time. Then, in an angry tone, He said, "Sinchyala itka divas khayaayla ghaatle aani malkat kapde dhonaas malaa saangitle, tar nahe mhantto Maajha maala te dhutlech payaje, parantu lookachi maja paaha" [Roughly Translated – Sinchya – an abuse was given food for so many days. And told to wash the dirty clothes. But he said 'No' and that he should wash his own clothes, but look at the fun people are having"]. Then, Baba beckoned Karnik to come near. Karnik went forward eagerly and embraced Baba's feet, covering them with kisses. Baba suddenly said, "Will you give Me dakshina?" Karnik looked at his son, who gave him 'sava rupaya' which Karnik placed in Baba's hands. Baba, on receiving the dakshina, danced with joy and love and started singing, "Hyane tar sava rupaye dila, rupaye sava dila, Shri Ram Parvardigar" [He gave Me sava rupaye. Look, rupaye sava he gave Me]. Baba said, "This is your own home and only I am here. Do come frequently Okay". So happy was Karnik, that there and then, he started repeating Baba's words so that he could remember them by heart. After receiving permission, he indeed wrote them down. Enroute, he pondered over Baba's words. Being poor, it was not feasible for him to visit Shirdi frequently. So, what did Baba mean? Then it dawned upon him that the message was to go to Nana, as there was no difference between Baba and Nana. On reaching Kalyan, he went straight to Nana's home and told him about everything that took place in Shirdi. Nana agreed with his interpretation and asked him to learn the *Ram Raksha Stotra*. Thence, Karnik went daily to Chandorkar's home for *satsang*.

A month later, his second son visited Shirdi along with his father. During aarti, Karnik, his son and Ram Maruti, who was there all stood together. Baba looked at Karnik and said, "For two thousand years, we have had a close relationship. From the very beginning, he was fond of joking".

After aarti, they went for Baba's darshan. Karnik however sat at a distance from Baba, who lovingly said, "Being a long-time friend, why this distance." Saying this, Baba beckoned him to come near and hugged him like a mother would. He then applied udi and placed His hand on Karnik's head. "Give Me six rupees dakshina," said Baba. Karnik asked his son who at once gave the amount. Baba then said, "The son who gives the money immediately, Allah will bless him". Then turning to Karnik, Baba said, "Do not hesitate to ask Me for anything you need." Then Karnik asked his son for dakshina and depleted him of all his money. At that juncture, a young solicitor came for darshan, and seeing Karnik, asked Baba to bless his aged father.

"My Grace is not partial. I bestow it on everyone equally, for not a leaf moves without My grace." Karnik heard these words and felt it was Baba's first lesson. On reaching Kalyan, he related everything to Nana who explained the *Isvayas Upanishad*.   [Ref: *Sai Leela*, No 4-5, Year 4, 1926]

Leela 3:   **Amidas Bhavani Mehta**

His samadhi is in the central part of Lendi Baug. Amrutlal was his real name. He was a Nagar Brahmin from Bhavnagar (Kathewad, Saurashtra). Amidas was from the community of Narsingh Mehta. He was an intellectual poet and a devotee of Lord Krishna. Daily with great devotion, he worshipped Lord Krishna. And every time he looked at his Lord's photograph, he saw a fakir superimposing his Lord in the glass.

He was perplexed to see a Muslim fakir superimposing Lord Krishna, and his curiosity was aroused. So, he set out to find this Fakir who was none other than Sai Baba of Shirdi. Amidas was a very learned man. He was trained in Indian classical and vocal music. He was affluent and was attached to a small king Dayashankar Revashankar Pandya in Kathewad. In those days, Kathewad was divided into small kingdoms, ruled by Gujarati Nawabs.

Being well off, he visited Shirdi frequently and rented a room there. Thus he was able to stay in Shirdi for long periods of time. He spent most of his time with Baba.

He started writing about Baba in Gujarati, and Baba's fame spread to Gujarat also. Amidas was a poet and his poetry was about the life, habits, likes and dislikes and characteristic of Sai Baba who was *Purna Parabrahma* to him. As he was in close contact with Baba he was able to write about His life and the book is titled *Purna Parabrahma Srisadgurusainath Maharajni - Janavajog Vigato Temaj Chamatkaro*.

Baba loved Amidas for his kind gentle nature. When somebody was sick in Shirdi, Baba would send him to Amidas. Amidas gladly tended to the patient with tender loving care and nursed him back to health. His wish was to die in Shirdi in the vicinity of his Guru. Baba knew his desire and said, "You may die anywhere, but you will always be with Me."

He breathed his last in Shirdi and hence his samadhi is there in Lendi Baug next to Muktaram's samadhi.

Leela 4: **Firozshah Hormazji Pudumjee**

The year was 1917. Firoz was in high school, when his parents made a pilgrimage to Shirdi. While returning, they brought a photograph of Baba as *prasad*. On returning home, the parents gave a glowing account of Baba's divinity to the family. Firoz heard all this and he wondered that, "They run after these babas and sadhus. Will this Sai Baba help them spiritually and materially?" He also put a test to Baba thinking, "If Baba is divine, He will give me a sign." With this thought, he went to sleep.

That night he dreamt of Baba who said, "You want proof of My divinity? Whether I am for real or not? Your father has placed My photograph on the table. When you get up in the morning, try and pick it up. If you can pick it up, I am fake. If you cannot pick it up. Know for sure that I am real." The dream awakened him, and he couldn't wait for dawn to break. In the morning, he went to the dining table and tried to pick up Baba's photograph. But the photograph was extremely heavy. The more he tried, the heavier it got. The table itself was lifted off the floor, but not the photograph. Then he realised that Baba was indeed divine.

Later, he started working in his father's mill gratis. One day, he dreamt of Baba, who said, "You have been working in your father's mill for so long. You need to get a salary." The next day, his uncle casually asked him if he was getting paid for all the work he was doing. On hearing the negative reply, his uncle started paying him two hundred rupees per month. Firoz did not meet Baba, but he was devoted to Him. He kept wondering, what Shirdi looked like? One day, while travelling by bus, he passed by Sai Baba lane in Santa Cruz. Intuitively, he knew that he would find his answer there. Later, he went to that lane and met Moreshwar Pradhan, who was very close to Baba. Pradhan readily and gladly answered all his questions in great detail, until he was satisfied.

[Ref: *Sai Leela*, 1928 April *(Chaitra)*]

Leela 5:   **Equality of Vision**

"I look at everyone with equality. Many people come to My durbar with different motives and needs. The people who are here, are also as different as different can be. Some are God-fearing. Some are seekers of knowledge and enlightenment. Others are seekers of wealth, health, and progeny. Others are rogues. Nonetheless I look at each and everyone with equality", said Baba.

Here are two such Leelas.

The year was 1913 and "Naam-Saptah" was being performed, by some of the devotees. The Dwarkamai was packed as devotees had gathered together, to participate in the weeklong programme. Savitri Bai Tendulkar was also present and so was Baba Sahib Tarkhad. Baba calmly said, "Go Shama, there is a man sitting against the wall of the Sabha Mandap. He wishes to have Darshan. Go and bring him up immediately". Shama did as he was bidden. Indeed, there was a man huddled next to the wall of Dwarkamai. But he was in a bad shape.

The man was not very old. But his hands were shaking and his head was nodding. He was drooling at the mouth. His body was full of boils that oozed pus. Some of the boils had turned to open sores that were full of maggots. Flies covered his chest. The torn clothes that he had on were filthy and dirty. There was an overpowering stench of foul odour.

Shama seemed oblivious of this, and holding the man by his hand, brought him to Baba. The man fell at Baba's feet and tears of joy poured from his eyes. Baba placed his hand of benediction on his head and said, "Bhau, what have you brought for Me?" This devotee's joy knew no bounds at that moment. Slowly and painstakingly, he took out a dirty piece of cloth and opened the bundle. Inside the bundle was a small piece of paper that had two to three pieces of sugar candy. With his shaking hands, he handed the candy to Baba with utter devotion. On receiving the candy, Baba gobbled it up. Then Baba placed his palm on his head and gave him udi and permission to leave. The man slowly but joyously left the Dwarkamai. Baba Sahib Tarkhad watched the whole scenario with keen interest and was so moved by Baba's compassion and love, that he could not hold back his tears.

[Ref: *Sai Leela*, Ank1-2, Year 8, 1930]

Leela 6:   **Munim and 2 ½ lakhs**

" All kinds of people come here, Vani, Teli, Varul, Kulkarni, and Tambolis do come here," said Baba to Ramachandra A. Tarkhad. It was Dussehra holidays in the year 1915. At about 2:30 in the afternoon, when Mahatara and his friend were doing Charanseva to Baba [Baba called Tarkhad as Mahatara]. The junior munim (manager) of his firm came for Baba's darshan. Both Jyotindra Tarkhad and the Munim looked at each other, aghast "Why are you anxious? Be calm and look at every act unfolding before you, unruffled and with detachment," said Baba. The munim was in a desperate state.

He looked starved, unshaven and unkempt. Anxiety was written all over his face. He bowed at Baba's feet, then touched Tarkhad's feet. Baba turning to Dixit (one of his devotee seated there) said, "Kaka take this man to your *wada* (a dwelling) and after a meal, let him come for Darshan". Kaka did as he was asked.

Tarkhad's mind was racing around in circles. He thought, "What am I to do? This man has gambled away two and a half lakhs of money of the cotton speculation and sales. The managing director of the firm has put out a police warrant for him. There is prize money for anyone who finds him. I cannot betray my manager, but he has sought refuge in Baba. My allegiance is to my manager, but my faith and devotion lies with Baba." Again Baba said, "Why are you so anxious?".

Meanwhile, the other devotees began questioning Tarkhad as to who that particular devotee was. He vaguely replied that he knew him from Bombay. But they were not satisfied. "What will I say when I meet my managing director?" he thought. "Should I tell him that he came to Shirdi." Baba reassured him again. The munim had a bath, and dined at Dixit's wada. Then the two of them came to the Dwarkamai. Baba expertly sent Dixit and Tarkhad to do some chore, and spoke to the munim alone. "Leave Shirdi at once and go to the manager and tell him what you have done and beg his pardon", said Baba.

The munim followed Baba's advice and went to Bombay after an absence of five months. Strangely, the manager asked the police to be lenient with the culprit. Baba had changed the mind and infused compassion into him. When Tarkhad reached Bombay, he told the manager what had happened, while he was at Shirdi. The manager wasn't upset with Tarkhad and assured him that everything would be all right. The munim had after all sought refuge in Baba.

Leela 7: **Uddhavesh alias
Shyamdas Baba**

He was born on 9th June, 1865 and took samadhi on 8th August 1951.

It was from Konkan prantha, Ratnagiri jilha, Devgad gaon that his ancestors hailed from. Then they moved to Thane, where Uddhavesh (photo 15 and 16) grew up. He was born on the ninth of June 1865. From early childhood, he was an ascetic by nature and loved to go on pilgrimages and visit saints and sadhus. He first visited Shirdi in 1904. This visit itself was very predictive of Baba's grace on him. He had undertaken an elaborate pilgrimage of Rameshwar; from Wardha, it was by foot. On taking Gajanan Maharaj's darshan, the saint told him to go south of Shegaon, where he would meet his Guru. Then, Harihar Baba at Shivlee who did not speak, except for saying Harihar, indicated that Uddhavesh would find his moksha Guru at a place that rhymed with Shivlee (Shiladi) in the westward direction.

At Shivlee, a party gave Uddhavesh a wild horse for his journey. The horse was bad natured for he bit you if you stood before him, and kicked you, if you stood behind him. Nonetheless, taking him along, he came to Ahmednagar jilha, 'the land of saints'. At Belapur, he had the darshan of Keshav Govind's samadhi and reached Kopargaon. After having bathed in the Godavari, he did *naamjap* and thence came to Shirdi.

In those days, Shirdi was a desolate place with abundant *babul* trees. He tied his horse to a babul tree. Taking care to muzzle his mouth and tying his hind legs to another tree, lest he may attack *wayfarers*. It was then that he noticed a fakir in a torn-tattered *kafni* (robe) with a tin tumrel (a pot used for collecting gravied food) in his hand, walking about aimlessly. He went up to him and politely asked him, where the Sadhu of Shirdi stayed. The fakir blessed him with a shower of abuses. This episode hurt him to the core and he made his way to the village. "He is an old cantecarous man and instead of answering a simple question in a civil manner, he abused me and my mother," he thought. On reaching the village, he came to the masjid. There was a hut next to it and an old lady was making *bhakar* and *pitla*. He enquired about the saint of Shirdi. She told him that He had gone out, but there was no saying as to when He would return. So, she was making bhakar ready for Him to eat whenever He would return. He enquired about His appearance. She described in great detail about Baba's torn tattered kafni and headgear.

The masjid was littered with garbage in front of it. But the inside was clean and neat. In a corner, there were four lighted lamps, next to it a hand-mill and some old and faded marigold garlands and some fresh garlands. A *dhuni* was burning in front of the pillar. He wondered about the lighted lamps and the entire set-up as he made his way back. The lady was a Hindu, the Sadhu described was a Muslim, and his mind was in a turmoil. "Agni in the Masjid! Why?" Many questions arose in his mind on his way back. There he saw Baba patting his horse. Baba had one hand in the horse's mouth and with the other hand He was patting his head.

Spontaneously, he said, "Be careful Maharaj! This is a wild creature and he bites viciously." He then went and laid his head on Baba's feet. He was filled with peace and he stood up and asked the burning question, "Maharaj, where and when will I find my Guru?" Still patting the horse, Baba answered, "Kallel pudhe, tu kothun aalas? Mee tar vedaa Fakir aahe" [You will realise in the future where you came from. I am but a mad Fakir]. Then He added, "After five years, everything will be clear. Okay. Go. Leave today and do upwas [Upwas here is indicative of *sadhana*]." Then Baba and Uddhavesh returned to the masjid. Some devotee had left a coconut offering. Baba broke it and gave half to Uddhavesh. Then He said, "Arre, how can a whole bhakar go down the stomach all at once. You will realise in five years. At that time, we will see." Then, Uddhavesh bowed to Baba and left for Kopargaon and joined the rest of the group and continued his pilgrimage.

Between 1906 and 1911, he was fortunate to meet Nana Chandorkar, Janardhan Gonddev Kandikar and Bala Sahib Dev, who told him many leelas of Sai Baba.

In 1906, he visited Shirdi and Baba said, "Come Shyamdas, it is good that you have come. Ghoda Baeel Chaavka. Aamasee bhet to paavka" [Roughly Translated – Horses and bulls bite. But when they meet Me, they become meek and gentle]. These words reminded him of Baba's divine presence which was perceived even by the vile horse. Harihar Baba had told Uddhavesh that he would find his Moksha guru at Shirdi. Every time he visited Shirdi, thence, he stayed for longer periods of time.

Once he had gone to Dwarkamai and found Baba grinding wheat. At that time, Baba had ground a little wheat and was about to grind some more. He went to the Sanctum Sanctorum and sat down and noted that Baba, while grinding was singing awhile, saying Vedanta awhile, then showering abuses. He was so fascinated by the grinding, that he asked Baba, "Baba, why have You kept this hand mill? Why do You do this chore of grinding?" Baba then said, "Ithe je yetaat, tyaanche malaa dalaava laagta bara [Whoever comes to Me I have to grind for them]. Thus he realised that Baba grounds the suffering and karmas of the devotees who come to Him. This sentence struck the core of his heart and he realised how much trouble and hardship Baba undergoes for us.

Our *sanchit* (the sum total of merit and demerit of the present life as well as all the previous births) and *kriyaman* (the actions of this present life with its repercussions and fruits in future births) are whirling around like a wheel. Then there are our hopes, aspirations, goals and trials. Only the Sadguru

15

shoulders our tribulations for material benefits. Finally, to set us on the path of spirituality, helping us as we take the first few steps like a mother carrying us every time we falter or fall. Only the Sadguru can liberate us from the cycle of future births and deaths. No one else can!

When he went to take permission to leave, he said, "Baba, why don't you call me more frequently to Shirdi?" Then Baba, turning to Bala Shimpi said, "He says I don't call him often. Yet we meet every fifteen days. Don't we?" Shyamdas had a routine of writing to Baba on Ekadashi of every month and Baba used to reply. Baba was referring to this. Then Baba, as usual, gave him a handful of *udi* and blessed him. In a motherly tone, Baba said, "So you are leaving? Arre Shyamdas, I am with you all the time Allah Ram Malik will bless you and do good. Okay."

On his last visit, he had gone to the Dwarkamai in the afternoon at about 3 o'clock. Some devotees were seated at the Sabha Mandap and they cautioned Shyamdas not to go to the Dwarkamai. Baba at that time was sitting still as if in meditation. Just then, one of the devotees went up for darshan. Baba flew into rage and swiftly smacked the devotee with his *satka*. He let out a volley of abuses. The devotee fled from the Dwarkamai. Shyamdas went up and Baba welcomed him as if nothing had happened. Shyamdas sat awhile and Baba said, "Shyamdas when will you come again?" Shyamdas replied that he would return quickly and taking udi, he left. He had not even reached the gate of the Sabha Mandap, when Baba called out to him. He retraced his steps and went to Baba. Baba said, "Henceforth, don't come to Shirdi Okay. I am always with you wherever you may be, Okay. The people here have changed a lot they trouble me incessantly with their cries for money [paisa] and I am getting tired. Are you going on a yatra, or are you going to meet your family. I am always with you now and forever."

Then Baba gave him the permission to go. Try as he may, he couldn't make a trip to Shirdi, nor could he send his letters on Ekadashi. Then Shyamdas received letters from various devotees informing him that Baba had taken Mahasamadhi.

[Ref: *Sai Leela*, Ank 4-5, Year 4, 1926]

Leela 8:   **Quenching the Thirst**

"**M**y Nana is in trouble. He is overcome by thirst. Should we not give him a palmful of water?" said Baba sitting in the Dwarkamai.

The Bhadranika Upanishad in Chapter three to seven, Shloka four says, "He who inhabits water, but is within it. Who water does not know. Whose body is water, and controls it from within. He is the internal ruler." Thus Baba could give water to a thirsty Nana, and Shyam Das on Girnar Parvat. He could also quieten and stop the storm that was in all its fury, when it rained in torrents at Shirdi [*Shri Sai Satcharita* – Chapter 11]. So also the production of water to wet His chappy (a piece of cloth placed around the chillum – clay pipe for smoking) at the meeting of Chand Bhai Patil [*Shri Sai Satcharita* – Chapter 5].

The rinanubandh for each devotee was different; but Baba's compassion, vigilant watchfulness and love were equal and infinite. Nana, though overweight, was very fond of visiting temples on hilltops. Harishchandra hill is forty miles away from Shirdi with a Devi temple on its summit. Once Nana Sahib Chandorkar (photo 37) with his entourage of peons and *sheristadars* made this pilgrimage. It was a hot summer day and the hill was rocky and barren. There were no trees for shade or water to drink. The troupe had climbed halfway, when Nana was fatigued and overcome by thirst. The provisions they had brought were exhausted. The Sheristadar suggested they return. But exhaustion and thirst had taken its toll and Nana could not do so.

He just sat on a flat slab of stone and said, "If Baba were here, He would surely give me water to slate my thirst." The Sheristadar thought that this speculation was futile as Baba wasn't there. But Baba was with Nana at all times.

Here at Shirdi, Baba said, "My Nana is in trouble." At that very moment, a Bhil was walking down the hill. Nana said, "I am very thirsty. Can I get some water to drink?" The Bhil replied, "What? You ask for water? Under the very slab on which you are seated, there is water." Then he walked on. The peons and sheristadars moved the slab and found a palm full of clear sparkling water; just enough to slate his burning thirst. Nana drank the water and having quenched his thirst, continued the pilgrimage. He took darshan of the goddess and returned home.

It is said that prayer is a concentrated one pointed contact with a higher power. When a devout soul is concentrating deeply on God, the soul gets thoroughly saturated with the divine and the divine power infiltrates the *jeeva* and produces certain results. Here, the mere thought of Baba had instantaneous results. The faith, devotion, and love behind the thought were the trigger of Baba's leela. Later, when Nana visited Shirdi, Baba said, "Nana you were thirsty. I gave you water. Did you drink it."? This increased Nana's faith further by leaps and bounds. He was convinced more than ever, that Baba was omnipresent, omnipotent, merciful and loving, that Baba had the power to bring water to the barren hill, then appear as the Bhil and save his life while He sat in the Dwarkamai with the devotees.

Tatya Sahib Nulkar (L.K.Nulkar), whom Baba lovingly called 'Mahatara' or old man, used to write to his friend and mentor Nana Sahib Chandorkar regularly. On 20/07/1909, Tatya writes, "What have I left to say to one, who's Guru remembers him every moment of the day. Day and night, he says, 'Nana, Nana' and 'Kaka, Kaka'."

Tatya gives us an insight of the love and the rinanubandh that Baba and Nana had for each other. While Nana replies, quoting a *doha* from Kabir which says, "Iron gets spoilt, when it comes in contact with a touchstone. When it gets spoilt, it turns into gold. I am so very glad to see I have succeeded in spoiling you by the Grace of Sai Maharaj. It is now for you to make efforts for a good progress." Further Nana writes, "It was a desire to sleep in the lap of the mother. The mother has fulfilled this desire. Now, the one who is, will be taken care of by her, but one must adhere to such practices that one dreams of mother and she always remains before one's eyes. Then, the mother (Guru Mauli) will rattle the name of Mahatara as she does Nana and Kaka. Have no doubt."

What a beautiful letter it is, so full of insight, understanding and love. Passionate love for the Guru Mauli.

Leela 9: **Shyamdas on Girnar Parvat**

As usual, Shyamdas set out on another pilgrimage to Dwarka, Porbandar, Girnar, Somnath and many holy kshetras taking about three and a half months to do so. He, along with a group of pilgrims and his personal servant stopped at Girnar parvat (hill). They chalked out a neat programme to climb the parvat and take darshan of the Dattatreya *padukas*, then Ambaji Tekdhi (Ambadevi Temple atop the hill), and Gorakshakarnath Temple. The day of the climb happened to be a Thursday. So, the group decided to have darshan first and then a meal. Although they had an early start, nonetheless, they were delayed and had got late.

Shyamdas while ascending the mountain, clearly heard Baba say, "I am always with you." Happily, he continued up the hill, where some thirty to forty steps were rather steep, high and difficult to negotiate. The heat of the day was intense, the sun was beating on him with full intensity and the water he had brought was over. Still, another two hundred to three hundred steps were in front of him. Shyamdas was four to five steps ahead of the group, when he felt extremely exhausted. His throat was parched, he felt dizzy and fell down. When the group reached him, they found that he had fallen to the left.

Had he fallen a bit to the right, there would have been no trace of him as there was a deep ravine. Quickly, Tarabai and the group came to his rescue. They found that he was unconscious, frothing at the mouth and had a heat stroke. Tarabai sat down next to him, and cradling his head in her lap, wiped his mouth and started fanning him with a piece of cloth. The groups huddled together and were wondering what to do. The dire need for water was evident and there was nothing around them, except the steps leading to the top. It was decided that someone would retrace their steps to the bottom of the hill and fetch some water.

Just as they looked in that direction, they saw a Gosavi with a huge tamba (pot) of water, making his way towards them. He addressed Tarabai and said, "Mother, give the child this water, sprinkle some on his head and face and he will come around." So saying, he handed over the pot, and further added, "Make sure he drinks all this water. I've some work to do and I will meet you when you return." Then he ascended the steps. Mechanically, they did just what he said and Shyamdas started coming around. He could see the Gosavi had ascended about twenty steps or so and then he disappeared. It took about an hour for him to fully recover and they proceeded on. They had a wonderful darshan of all the temples. Meanwhile, the group was talking amongst themselves. "Who was this Gosavi? Why and how did he bring the water for Shyamdas? How specific were his instructions?" Shyamdas however knew that Baba had saved his life. Had not Baba assured him, saying, "I stand behind and in front of you, always and at all times." Where is Shirdi and where is Girnar? Yet the Guru Mauli is always at hand to help her child. When they returned to that very spot, he wished to wait for the Gosavi.

He did so for about an hour. But the group urged him to continue the descent. It was getting late, as it was now five p.m. and it would soon become dusk. Also, everyone was tired and hungry. Reluctantly, Shyamdas agreed and they reached the bottom of the hill at Junagadh Gaon. They had a meal and retired for the night.

But Shyamdas could not sleep. He was overwhelmed by what had happened. He had sustained no injury from the fall, except a few scratches and a grazed knee. Now, he was quite lucid and mentally all right, but he could not bare the thought of not having met his benefactor, the Gosavi. "Why?" he wondered. That night, he cried himself to sleep. That night, at about 4 a.m. in the morning, he had a vision. Baba said, "Arre Shyamdas, don't cry like this. There is a lot of work to be done. You will know in the future. Now get up." Shyamdas was comforted, as he was enveloped in Baba's love and concern for him. After some months, he came to Shirdi. As soon as he entered Dwarkamai, Baba said, "Come Shyamdas, didn't I give you a lot of water to quench your thirst?" Shyamdas went and laid his head on Baba's feet and washed them with tears. Baba placed His palm of benediction on his head and gave him udi.   [Ref: *Sai Leela*, Ank 4-5, Year 4, 1926]

Leela 10: **Ramachandra Atmaram Tarkhad**

The rough tumble and turmoil of worldly life was taking its toll on him. So, Ramachandra Atmaram Tarkhad decided to take a break and go to Shirdi.

He planned to spend a few days there at Baba's feet, get rejuvenated and return home. Leaving his family behind, he went with his friend to Shirdi. It was 6th December, 1910.

After spending about eleven hours in the train, he reached Kopergaon. He bathed in the Godavari and reached Shirdi by *tonga*. They alighted at Sathe Wada at about 9 a.m. The habit of having a cup of tea in the morning and its absence was felt by him. Nonetheless, he went to Sathe Wada and kept his belongings. When he was accosted by a Sadhu in a pink kafni, who said, "Aho Baba Sahib, why have you come to Shirdi? What do you get here? Because educated people like you come here, many people are flocking here for no good reason." Tarkhad was taken aback by what he said. But what upset him most was his tone of voice. It was full of disgust and ridicule. Before he could say anything, another sadhu in a white dress, holding a small stick with flowers tied to one end stood in front of him. He literally shouted in his ear, "What is the meaning of 'Stithaprajna'? (A man of serene wisdom). Please tell me in detail who is a Stithaprajna." By now, Tarkhad had lost his cool and was completely agitated. He wondered why he had come to Shirdi. He decided that he would go for Baba's darshan and take permission to return to Bombay that very day.

Just then, Bala Sahib Bhate came with a glass of piping hot tea and handed it to him and told him that his luggage would be taken care of while he went for darshan.

By now, Tarkhad had had enough and his mind was in a turmoil and he felt he was better off in Bombay. Trying to compose himself, he walked slowly to the Dwarkamai and laid his head on Baba's feet. Baba placed His beneficent hand on his head and said, "Why does he do this? Shama, take him to the Wada and tell him something."

The two walked out of the Dwarkamai and Shama asked Tarkhad why he was agitated and anxious. Tarkhad told him everything that had happened since he left Bombay, and that his mind, instead of gaining calm and peace was in turmoil. Shama said, "This is Baba's Leela. There is a lesson in all of this and he is showing you the answer. That is, that even in the midst of trials and tribulations, pressure of work, ups and downs of family life, one should not lose one's balance, but direct it towards God." They retraced their steps, and as soon as they entered the Dwarkamai, Baba said, "Bhau pay heed to Shama's words." Tarkhad took Baba's advice and he used this leela as his motto and was quite unruffled by calamities and financial difficulties. His faith in Baba and this advice worked like a charm for him. [Ref: *Sai Leela*, Ank 1-2, Year 1930]

Leela 11: **Three Annas Became One Lakh Rupees**

His life on the surface seemed full of misery and immense tribulation. But, when Baba's Grace is showered, even three *annas* become one lakh. Baburao Borawke lived in Saswad near Pune. His parents died when he was but a child. His uncle and other relatives took advantage of this unfortunate incident and misappropriated his father's property and squandered all the money, leaving Baburao penniless. So hard up for money was he that he had to give up schooling and look for employment. One of his maternal uncles lived in Shirdi. He had sugarcane fields and farms and made jaggery out of it.

The uncle was devoted to Baba and often spoke of Baba's leelas to Baburao. Baburao soon became a devotee and was eager to have Baba's darshan. Somehow, he managed to buy a ticket to Kopargaon, enroute to Shirdi. At Ahmednagar station, he decided to fast until he had Baba's darshan. At Kopargaon, he alighted and travelled three miles by tonga, up to the banks of the Godavari. When he realised he had only three annas left in his pocket and that was insufficient to take him to Shirdi, he decided to walk the rest of the way.

As his maternal uncle's home was on the way, he visited his home. His aunt requested him to have a meal and then proceed to Shirdi. He told her of his determination to have Baba's darshan first and then have a meal. Saying so he walked to Shirdi. Near Lendi, he met his uncle, who also invited him for a meal. Baburao was however eager to see Baba first. His uncle gave him one rupee and requested him to have a meal with the money. He accepted the rupee and went to the masjid. His heart was filled with joy and bliss upon beholding Baba's luminous form. He rushed up the steps of the Dwarkamai and laid his head on Baba's feet. Baba made him sit near Him and spoke to him kindly. Then, Baba asked for dakshina. Baburao told Baba about his hopeless situation and his inability to give dakshina. "Look in your pocket. Why keep the one rupee?" said Baba. Baburao thrust his hand in his pocket and took out the rupee bill that he had quite forgotten about, and offered it to Baba.

The wonderful experience that he had made him determined to stay in Shirdi. He worked hard in his uncle's field and daily took Baba's darshan. His hard work bore fruit and the harvest was extremely good. So, there was a great deal of jaggery that was sold for a profit. Baburao handed over all the money he made over to his uncle. One day, a friend of his uncle's visited them. He was extremely surprised to see his field. "How did you manage to transform this parched land into such a lush field?" he asked. The uncle pointed to his nephew and told him, that it was all his hard work. The friend asked Baburao whether he would join him as a partner. Baburao agreed.

Daily, he would tend to his uncle's field, then go to Kopargaon and work there till dusk. His hard work earned him one lakh rupees at the end of the year. Baburao, who had come to Shirdi with three annas in his pocket, was now a millionaire. He felt, it was only by Baba's grace that this had happened. He bought a house in a village nearby and came to Shirdi daily for Baba's darshan.

Leela 12: **Krishnaji Kashinath Joshi (Kusha Bhau)**

Baba beat him, shouting foul abuses at him. But he was overjoyed at having got Baba's '*uchchista*' [The leftovers of the food eaten] as prasad. Kusha Bhau (photo 13) had fasted on one Ekadashi day, when Baba asked him what he had eaten. He replied, "We eat nothing on Ekadashi except Kandmul (Potatoes, Sweet Potatoes and Tuber Vegetables)." Baba jokingly said, "You ate kaanda [onions]", phonetically prolonging the 'a' sound to mean onions. Orthodox Brahmins do not even touch onions on Ekadashi, let alone eat. Then Baba picked up some onions and forced him to eat them. Bhau said he would eat them only if Baba also joined him in the repast. So, both of them started eating onions. Just then, a group of devotees arrived in the Dwarkamai. Turning to them,

Baba said, "Look at this orthodox Brahmin eating onions today." Kusha Bhau said, "Baba asked me to eat them, and so did He."

At that time, Baba regurgitated and spat out something. And instead of onions, sweet potatoes were found. Kusha Bhau, not losing a moment, fell upon it and ate it. It was then that Baba beat him. Then Baba blessed him and said, "Henceforth, you just think of Me and stretch your palms, and it will be full of warm Udi from My Dhuni. This you should use to heal and cure diseases, and benefit people". And so he did. (Ref: *Devotees Experience*, Page 206)

Kashinath Pant [his father] hailed from Mezagaon district, Ahmednagar. He was a learned Brahmin, who spent his life doing various social service activities, like looking after the sick and helping the poor. He was also a spiritual person. In 1872, a son was born to him whom he named Krishna. Krishna, like his father was a very spiritual child. Right from childhood, he was interested in listening to mythological stories. He visited all the temples of his village, read the holy scriptures and recited various mantras. There was a Maruti Mandir in the village and Krishna went daily to that temple and did *puja* there.

One day, while going to the temple, he saw a Sadhu seated there. The Sadhu had a bright aura around him and was clothed in tiger-skin. After doing namaskar and puja to Maruti, he also did Namaskar to the Sadhu. The Sadhu was Vakratunda Maharaj. He beckoned to Krishna and asked him to sit beside him. Krishna did so and the Sadhu told him some religious stories. The Maharaj did not eat anything but lived on milk alone. Every day, he would give Krishna money and ask him to fetch the milk. Krishna happily obliged. One day, Krishna brought the milk but did not return the change. The next day, Maharaj asked him what he had done with the change.

Pat came the reply, "I bought *pedas* with the money and ate them." *Vakratunda Maharaj* smiled at him and said, "See that tree a short distance from here. Go there, and you will find a stone, beneath which is a pot. Open it and eat."

Krishna did what he was told, and indeed, there was a vessel full of pedas. He ate to his heart's content. Then he kept the vessel in its place and covered it as before. That night, the Sadhu was leaving Mezagaon, and Krishna accompanied him. The sadhu and shishya travelled far and wide and Vakratunda Maharaj bestowed all the *siddhis* that he had on Krishna. But Krishna wasn't satisfied. He wanted to learn mantras that would create spells and break spells, exorcising devils and invoking them. His Guru was very reluctant to teach him this. But Krishna was persistent and pestered him. The guru finally gave in. He wore the iron bangle and did the necessary rites and gained these negative siddhis too.

At that time he was about twenty-two years old. His Guru then bade him farewell and left him in Baba's custody. "Go to Shirdi, my brother. Sai Baba will look after you and guide you henceforth." So saying, he went to the Himalayas and took Samadhi there.

Kusha Bhau came to Shirdi but Baba shouted at him saying, "Throw that iron bangle in the Godavari." Till he did so and stopped the production of pedas by tantric means. Baba did not allow him to come to the Dwarkamai. He made him sit in a corner and read Dasbodha and other religious books. Kusha Bhau stayed with Baba for three years and gained a lot of spirituality. Baba asked him to get married. Though married, he would often come and stay in Shirdi.

On one of his visits, Baba said, " Why do you take the trouble to come all this distance to see Me? I am there." Baba then gave him a description of a particular plot of land, where He was. Kusha Bhau bought that land and clearing the rubble and shrubs found a samadhi. This was the samadhi of Hazrat Fakir Shah. Kusha Bhau used to go to the samadhi quite often and it was here only Baba gave him *sakshatkar* (appear in human form).

Kusha Bhau, under Baba's guidance gained a lot of spirituality and with it came a lot of siddhis. These siddhis he used judiciously to help humanity. He stopped using mantras to produce pedas and cast spells, as he used to do in his earlier days.

'Baba's prachar' became his mission and he went from place to place doing *bhajans, aarti* and curing various illnesses with Baba's *udi.* He had many disciples. His prime disciple was V.R.Kulkarni. Kusha Bhau's *ishta devta* was Dattatreya. Every year, he would go to his *gaon* (village) and celebrate Datta Jayanti with great zeal. Pune was the city that Kusha Bhau chose to reside in. Partly because his disciples were there and because he wanted to take samadhi there. He saw to it that his disciples were devoted to Datta and Baba.

In Maagh (February) on dashmi [tenth day], Saturday, 1944, he took samadhi. Before his death he gave instructions to Kulkarni and other disciples about his samadhi. His samadhi (photo 14) is in Parvati, Poona, housed in the temple. As you enter the temple, there is a samadhi, atop which there is a *murti* of Dattatreya and Sai Baba. It was Kusha Bhau's desire that the water from the *abhishekh* of his ishta dev Dattatreya and his Sadguru Sai Baba should flow over the samadhi.

His disciples who formed the Sadguru Das Kisen Sai Baba Mandal fulfilled his wishes. Kusha Bhau's samadhi in the *temple* is famous in Poona for two reasons. First, it is believed that anyone who does seva here will have all his or her wishes fulfilled. Secondly this temple is famous because on the marble top of the Samadhi, Baba gave *sakshatkar* (appear in human form).

[Ref: *Shri Krishnanath Maharaj Yacha Parichay.* Published by VR Kulkarni. at Shri Krishnanath Dutt Mandir]

Leela 13: Shyamdas and Dwarka

A group of pilgrims along with Shyamdas set out to Dwarka by a steamer. Shyamdas had the tickets for the steamer along with his money in a purse. Later he kept the tickets in his pocket. That evening, while he stood at the railing of the steamer, his purse accidentally fell into the sea. The officials of the steamer when told about it, were considerate, as he had tickets for the onward journey. But, having no money posed a problem. That night, Gopal Giridhar [his son] had a vivid dream. A fakir came into his bedroom and awakened him by shaking him. "Send money to your father at Dwarka," he said. Giridhar looked around but found nobody. Then he fell asleep again. Again, the same fakir appeared and rather angrily said, "I told you to send money to your father. He is stranded there, while you are sleeping." This time he got up and went to the door to look for the fakir. But the door was locked and there was no fakir anywhere.

He sat up and thought over the dream, then realised that his father must be in trouble and stranded at Dwarka. That very day he had received some money from an insurance company. He decided to send that money to Shyamdas. He waited anxiously for daybreak and then sent him fifty rupees. Shyamdas was pleasantly surprised to receive the money and completed the pilgrimage with ease. On returning from Dwarka he met Giridhar and asked him how he managed to send the money at the opportune moment. Giridhar related the leela in vivid detail.

When Shyamdas went to Shirdi at Kopargaon, he had some difficulty at getting a *tonga*. But as soon as he finished his ritual of bathing in the Godavari doing *jap* and *puja* at the

29

Datta Mandir a tonga with two passengers stopped before the mandir. The passengers asked him to accompany them because the third passenger could not make this trip to Shirdi. On reaching Shirdi the tonga driver asked Shyamdas for one rupee fare, and not the customary five rupees. Shyamdas went to Dwarkamai for 'Dhule' darshan. He found Baba sitting with Butti, Bala Sahib Bhate, Chinchanikar and some other *bhaktas*. Baba was sitting near the railing and was handing Bade Baba a *chillum*, when He saw Shyamdas. Just then Shama said, "Deva, see, Shyamdas has come for your Darshan." Then Baba said, "I've been looking after him for a long time, and will look after him in the future too." Then Baba added, "Shyamdas, you drowned the money in the sea. Allah Malik gave you money. He also gave you water to drink." Shyamdas was overwhelmed by Baba's love and care. He went and laid his head on Baba's feet for about fifteen minutes. Then, Baba patted his head and said, "Get up Shyamdas, sit awhile with Me." Baba's grace enveloped Shyamdas and continued even in the later part of his life.   [Ref: *Sai Leela,* Ank 4-5, Year 4, 1926]

While on the pilgrimage to Dwarka, Shyamdas was reading Atwala's *Dnyaneshwari.* His purse along with the tickets had fallen into the sea. That day he couldn't concentrate on the chapter and read it rather mechanically. It was then that he took a negative decision. "I will not read any scripture till Baba tells me to." After his trip, he came to Shirdi. At that time, Baba did not ask for dakshina, nor did he give any. The subject of reading any religious books did not arise and he returned home. He wrote letters to Baba on *(ekadashi)*, and received a reply. Thus, two to three years passed. Once, Chidambar Keshav Gadgil read out Shyamdas' letter to Baba. Baba said, "Call him here. Ask him to come quickly."

Shyamdas went to Shirdi within four days of receiving the reply. Baba asked him daily for eleven rupees that he readily gave, daily for ten days. Every day, he would go to Dwarkamai at about 3:30 in the afternoon and only at that time would Baba ask for dakshina. On the eleventh day, as usual, Baba asked for dakshina. Shyamdas had no money left. He said, "Baba, I've no money left to give You as dakshina. You tell me, where am I to get the money from?. In lieu, I offer my ten Indriyas and mind". To this Baba replied, "They are mine already. Who are you to give them? Go to Bapu Sahib Butti and borrow 11 Rs. And give them to Me." On hearing this, Shyamdas got up to go and got the money. He had hardly reached the gate of the Sabha Mandap, when Baba called out to him, " Arre Shyam come here, and bring the eleven rupees later. But bring them from Bapu Sahib Jog. Now be seated." After taking *udi* and prasad he went to the *wada* and totally forgot about the eleven rupees. At 3:30 he went for darshan, but Baba did not ask for the eleven rupees. In the evening he said, " Go to Bapu Sahib Jog and ask for eleven rupees and bring him along with you."

Shyamdas went to the Wada and found Baba Sahib Jog reading the *Eknath Bhagwad* to a few devotees. He told Jog what Baba had said. Both of them went to the masjid. Baba was getting ready to go out. On seeing them He blessed them, but did not ask for dakshina. Later they returned to the Wada. The other devotees asked Shyamdas about this episode of 'eleven rupees dakshina and what it meant. Shyamdas had not pondered over it. Every day, thereafter, both of them went to Baba, but Baba did not ask for dakshina.

On the fourth day, it was in the evening, when Baba asked Jog, "So, how many rupees did you distribute today". Jog replied, "Sixty-one rupees. Butti received fifty rupees and Shyamdas eleven." Shyamdas was silent all this time when Baba said, " Did you get the eleven rupees?" Without understanding its significance, Shyamdas said "yes". Then Baba said, "No, you didn't. Let us see tomorrow. In the meantime, have a look at the Pothi, okay?" They returned to the wada and started discussing what Baba could have meant by asking for eleven rupees. Bala Sahib Bhate was astute enough to connect the dakshina with the reading of *Eknath Bhagwad*. Suddenly, Shyamdas remembered how he had taken a decision not to read any pothi, unless directed by Baba to do so. Later, he went to the Masjid, and Baba told them a long story that is given below.

"We were two brothers on a long journey. While walking on a path, my brother went ahead. He was bitten by a serpent and died. I was walking steadily and was way behind him. Just then five to six people came and enquired of me, where my brother was? I told them he had died due to a snakebite. And I had buried him. They did not believe me. "We will go and search for him and bring him back," they said. I cautioned them saying, "There is a huge serpent there. It will bite you too. "Why are you going there?" But they did not pay heed to My words. They did go there and were killed by the serpent. I buried them also and continued My journey.

"Then, a strong lady came and asked where my brother was? I told her that a huge serpent bit him, hence he died and was buried by me. Then she enquired about the six men. I told her how they went looking for the brother, and were killed by the serpent. She was anxious to go there and find my brother. I said, "Why are you going there needlessly. You will not find my brother" To that she, replied, "I will go there and diligently search for him, find him and bring him back." Thus she went ahead, she too met the same fate. I buried her too. Then I continued my journey. And went a long distance. Then I met five to six Muslims who said, "Wait awhile." I waited. They brought a goat, killed it and cut it into pieces. These they brought to me and said "Eat". I said, "No, I am a Brahmin and I cannot eat it". When one of them took a piece, and thrust it towards my lips, trying to make me eat it, I said, " Just wait awhile, I will pray to God then eat it". I took a piece of cloth and held it to my mouth and thought of God, Lo! The pieces of meat turned into roses. Huge beautiful roses, that you couldn't find anywhere, even in Shirdi. Then those Muslims went away. I continued my journey. When I looked back there was water, crystal clear, and a small pathway ahead. I walked a short distance. And there was water on either side, behind and in front of me, without any pathway. This is the doing of Allah Malik. Allah Malik is the saviour of the poor".

It is very difficult to know the meaning of Baba's words and parables. Only the devotee for whom it was meant could comprehend its meaning. The possible meaning is given below.

The two brothers on a long journey symbolise 'the real I' or the atma or soul and the other brother is 'the apparent I' identified with the body, mind, senses, intellect that is the 'psycho physical matter.' Having been identified with these the 'apparent I' suffers from pain and pleasure. To release the 'apparent I' from this cycle, one has to 'bury' it mercilessly. Here Baba suggests the mode of burying by practising Yoga.

Bitten by the serpent and having died symbolises the burial of the 'apparent I' by awakening the kundalini. Yogic path teaches the gradual uncoiling of the kundalini, which is a spiritual current. As it uncoils and rises upwards it enfranchises a series of *chakras*. The six chakras are known for their own powers and at last culminate in sahasara or the thousand petalled Padma in the brain followed by Samadhi *Sthiti* (state). But this state is not for long as the *vasanas* are not destroyed completely.

Baba mentions five to six people possibly symbolising the vasanas governed by five *panchindrias* and six *arishadvargas*. When these evils continue their attack by luring the real sadaka he is neither frightened nor affected. On the other hand "They will also be buried by him". Thus Baba's statement that "there is a huge serpent, and I buried him, and the journey" symbolises the burial of vasanas.

The "strong lady" referred here symbolises maya (illusion). Due to ignorance the Real Self is forgotten. One then starts identifying with the Apparent Self. Thus one is entangled in this worldly life and such experiences as birth and death, pain and pleasure, and good and evil. All these seem so real, though the waking stage and the dream stages are both a mirage. This Maya veils the pure soul and has to be buried in order to realise the pure soul or atma. Baba's statement confirms that

33

He has buried maya by stating that the strong lady met the same fate and was buried. Still the vasanas continue attacking. This is symbolically stated as five to six people "cutting the goat and thrusting the pieces on the lips". So strong are the vasanas or maya.

The word Brahmin refers not to the caste, but to the person who has realised "brahman." And because of the knowledge of brahman he is able to convert the pieces of meat into beautiful roses. This symbolises converting vasanas into knowledge.

"The crystal clear water and a small pathway" is the clarity the sadhaka attains by way of Sadhana to be with "Parabrahma" Then there is water all around him without any pathway which symbolises the highest state of realisation – the state of pure consciousness. Thus the sadhaka culminates with the Parabrahma.

The next day, Baba was in a tearing rage right from early morning till noon. Some of his devotees received his wrath in the form of beatings and abuses. But His daily routine went on as usual. Shyamdas went to the Dwarkamai at 3:30 p.m. and did charanseva. Baba said, "You received the eleven rupees, didn't you Shyam?" To which he replied, "If the eleven rupees is regarding the reading of the pothi, then yes. But which pothi am I supposed to read. Then, Baba gave a clue of the *rinanubandh* of theirs, saying, "Read that Pothi where there is a dialogue (Karmic ties or debts) between you and Me". This sentence further confused him. Should he read *Gita* or *Dnyaneshwari?* Baba said, "Arre Shyamdas, go to Bapu Sahib Jog and bring the Pothi that he is reading." He did so and Baba opened randomly the eleventh chapter of *Eknath Bhagwad* and pointing to it said, "Read this, every day of your life. Read it just as it is written and understand it for yourself. Do not explain or expound it to other people. Only you need to know and understand it. Allah Malik will do good."

Leela 14:   **Ramachandra Dada Patil**

How great was the *rinanubandh of* these two? Their love was deep and unfathomable! Ramachandra was born in Shirdi. He was the only son of Radhabai and Dada Kote Patil. Ramachandra had three sisters. He was born to affluence. His ancestral property spread far and wide in Shirdi and neighbouring villages. His father owned many acres of farm land which yielded all types of grain and sugarcane. Hence he had to only supervise the labourers.

Ramachandra (photo 65) was a very bright student and he studied up to seventh standard in Marathi. But most of all he was interested in the legal system He was responsible for incorporating the village of Beragaon into Shirdi [Maruti Mandir has two *vighras* one for Shirdi and one for Beragaon]. It is said that in those days the boundary of Shirdi was up to the Chavadi beyond which was Beragaon.

He was the secretary of Dakshina Bhiksha Sanstha. He started doing Baba's seva at the tender age of 11 years. He had immense faith in Baba and took Baba's word as law. In 1916, he was extremely sick with influenza [Ref: *Sai Satcharita* – Chapter 42]. Baba gave him *sakshatkar* and said "Tu gabro nakos, tula pushkal aayuse ahaya" [Don't be afraid you have a long life ahead of you]. Ramachandra was greatly relieved to hear this and he immediately asked about his friend Tatya. Baba however said, "Two years from today Tatya's death will occur; but don't tell this to anyone!" Ramachandra did recover but was terribly upset with what Baba said. So he confided in Bala Shimpi who was a good friend of his. Tatya was a dear friend of his since childhood.

They grew up together. Baba strengthened this bond between them 'by making them eat out of the same plate' daily in the Dwarkamai.

Ramachandra was married to Sitabai but as she had no children, he remarried and had two sons. After Baba's Mahasamadhi the devotees were working the whole night to get the Samadhi ready. Mir Shakar, a phelwan [body-builder] of Kohrale saw the developments and went to Appaji Kote Patil, who was Ramachandra's grandfather and managed to convince him that it was bad for the village to keep a dead body in it. He said, "Besides they were going to build the samadhi in Butti Wada. So they would get a Brahmin priest of their choice. Then they could lock the building and Muslims would not be able to enter". This appealed to Appaji and he called a meeting and told the villagers his views. Then the villagers agreed to take the body out of Shirdi.

Ramachandra heard this and disagreed saying that Baba's last wish should be followed and honoured. This enraged Appaji and he told him not to step into his house again. Ramachandra agreed as he was determined to honour Baba's wish at any cost. Indeed he did not enter his grandfather's residence for 12 years. Although his first wife Sitabai resided there. Tatya was well revered in the village and he sided with Ramachandra. The villagers met again but there was a split, a few people agreed with Appaji. But most of the younger villagers were adamant to honour Baba's wish. Single handedly Ramachandra set out to convince the devotees that had gathered in Shirdi for Baba's Mahasamadhi, about the importance of honouring Baba's last wish and he succeed. For 36 hours the body lay in Dwarkamai. At 4 p.m. on Thursday the body was placed in the Samadhi after a grand merunik [procession] through the village. On the thirteenth day Ramachandra arranged for a feast. The devotees distributed laddus to thousands of devotees and wonder of wonders happened. The number of *laddus* remained same after every distribution. Thus for two months laddus were distributed to every devotee.

Butti was extremely fond of Ramachandra, and he often invited him to Nagpur. Butti asked him to stay with him and help him with his business, but Ramachandra could not bear the thought of leaving Shirdi.

Ramachandra was sarpanj [head official] of the Shirdi Gram Panchayat for 20 years. The Nagar Palika has a photograph of his hanging in their office. Along with these duties he actively participated in the Shirdi Sai Baba Sansthan, and was the joint secretary for a long time. Ramachandra would get up early in the morning and have a cup of tea, after that he would eat nothing till the afternoon aarti. He attended the Aarti daily. Never sick for a single day. He died at the age of seventy. That day he had invited some guests for lunch. They were late in coming so his family suggested that he have lunch. He replied that he would wait for the noon Aarti . He sat down, as he was feeling giddy. Before they could seek medical help, he quietly and peacefully breathed his last. His descendents still live in Shirdi.

I for one have a special place in my heart for this great devotee. And I am eternally grateful to him and Gopal Rao Butti for gifting us the Samadhi and Samadhi Mandir.

Dwarkamai and Baba

"Hech Aapuli Dwaraka Matha! Mashidiche ye aaki baisatha lekhru dehi nirbhaysth" [Roughly Translated – This is our Dwaraka matha. The children who come; and sit in this Masjid should have no fear]. Baba said that His Dwarkamai was "mota kripalu" [tremendously compassionate] and the bhakta could easily cross the ocean [*beda paar*] of life. It was Baba who perceived the desires and longings of the devotees and granted their wishes.

Dr Keshav Gavankar in his book titled *Shiladhi* gives the meaning of 'Masjid'. He breaks down the word as 'Ma- Shi-Da'. To mean – Ma, is 'Mahan' [lofty], Shi – Shiv Paad [the feet of Shiva or the feet of Sai Baba], and Da – 'Deynari Jagha' [the place that gives]. So it means that great or lofty place where the feet of Lord Sai Baba is. And it was in this Masjid that the 'Sat- Chit-Anand Baba stayed, in bliss, and met His devotees.

It was from this Dwaraka Matha that Baba performed His leelas for 60 years and beyond. Baba often told His devotees that He was here thousands of years ago!. The old masjid was in a dilapidated condition and was about fifteen feet by seventeen feet]. This sanctified place with its contents can teach us many valuable lessons. Baba's life itself is an example of the highest truth that all religious teachings are the same .On the other hand Baba taught by example. He gave no sermons; nor preached to His devotees. A word here or a sentence there was sufficient to push the devotee to the next stage of his spiritual development.

Let me try to decipher the meanings and symbols of 'The Dwarkamai and Baba's sojourn in Shirdi' – The king of this universe. He who made this cosmos live in this dilapidated mosque. From where even the lizards ran away and took refuge elsewhere. Thus implying that only a roof is necessary to give us protection from the elements. And one does not need a huge palatial building to live in. As one enters the Sanctum Sanctorum; one finds Baba sitting 'facing the South, He is Dakshinamoorty'. This 'South faced guru symbolises the fact that a man of realisation has transcended time. That the Guru's Grace [as His inner realisation] is being showered on the devotees who are caught in the net of Yama, the lord of death. The guru leads the disciple to immortality. The south is the special domain of Yama. Yama means control. It can be self-control as well as a limitation over one's capacity.

Baba's asana [seat] was a sack. In the sack the weave is very evident, there is a horizontal weave. This symbolises man's life of hopes, aspirations, goals and greed for a thousand materialistic things. The vertical weave is the Sadguru's or God's will. The intersections as it were are milestones in one's life, when the devotee achieved or did not achieve his goal. This represents the essence of life.

We wish for thousands of things, but the result depends on His wish. And we should happily receive what He gives us. Sai Sharan Anand says, "The fabric of life should be woven with the woof of knowledge [*jnana*] and the weft of devotion [*bhakti*]. Unless jnana and bhakti are harmonised japa and other spiritual practises are incomplete"

Baba sat in the north-east corner, the direction of *Isana*. His left hand resting on the railing [Kathada]. His legs outstretched, showering His blessings on the devotees. There are eight directions or quarters in this world. Each protected by a Deity [*dikpals*]. Baba sat in the north-east corner which is protected by Isana on Vrishaba [Ox]. This symbolises that each individual goes a certain direction or follows a certain path that makes or mars his life, according to his vasanas. It is Lord Isana who guides the world. He comes riding on the Vrishaba to exhaust the accumulated vasanas of the *jeevas*. Thus Baba sitting in the north-east guides the individual in the right direction. Therefore any puja starts with "Astha Dik Bandhan" [The Eight Direction Bondage] and only then the mind of the individual is arrested from taking any direction. He discovers his own true nature.

The floor of the Dwarkamai was clean and neat. It was washed daily. Then slurry of cow dung was applied. Baba had an *akhand deep* [an ever burning lamp] which symbolises an inner light. Baba got up very early in the morning in *Bhrama Murth*. When the devotees came they found Him sitting in front of Dhuni Maa [Agni means leading towards evolution – Ref: *Nirukti*]. Fire is death to everything and water is death to fire.

If there are sins that are not burnt; then water will destroy them as it destroys fire. It means that one should burn the internal Dhuni and offer greed and desires as oblations. In *Bhadrinayka Upanishad's*, Chapter two, fifth shloka, *ovi* nine to fourteen, "God offered Faith as an oblation to fire [or *havan*] hence came the moon."

Baba went to Lendi Baugh twice a day. Lendi Baugh represents a garden with a multitude of shrubs of different varieties along with weeds. Baba went in procession up to Lendi Baugh but entered the Baugh alone. There like a gardener He tended to the plants and nurtured them [His devotees]. The weeds symbolise the various destructive tendencies that take hold of our lives and pull us in a different direction. When Baba went to Lendi Baugh, he threw water in four directions. Baba would sit facing west – the domain of Varun or rain. Varun means '*choicest things*' and also veiling or Maya [*Nirukti,* chapter ten [third stanza]. Varun is on *Makara* [crocodile] which is the hand of time.

The *nimbar* is on the Eastern wall and represents Mecca and Muslims do *namaz* facing it. However, Baba sat with His back to it during meal time. It was garlanded by the devotees daily. Thus one learns that all religions lead to the same goal or as Baba puts it succinctly '*Sub Ka Malik Ek.*' Even today the pujari of Dwarkamai garlands it.

Next to the *nimbar* is the '*jaath*' (quern or hand mill]. In Chapter 1 of *Shri Sai Satcharita* the wonderful leela of Baba grinding the wheat is given. Every day Baba undertook the chore of grinding the sins – the mental, the physical afflictions and the miseries of His devotees.

The quern has two grinding stones. The upper stone symbolises Bhakti [devotion] and the lower stone karma (deed) while the handle is *jnana* (knowledge). One has to grind all desires, sins, the traits of Raja, Tama, Ahamkar to develop spiritually. Through *bhakti* [faith], *nishwarth* [selfless], *karma* and of course the grace of the Sad Guru, and '*jnana*' the goal can be achieved.

Baba had but a few belongings that were kept in the Dwarkamai. These were:

(i) The Matka [Water pot]

It is an earthen vessel used for storing water. The mud pot symbolises the body that can break or die any time. Thus the transient or temporary nature of the human life. Water represents the *atma* [soul], which is the life-giving element to the body. Water is odourless, shapeless, colourless so also the soul. It is *nirlingi* [genderless], *nirlaptha* [not affected by anything], *nirvikari* [formless]. Being so, it will take the identity of any living being just as the water takes the shape of the container. The lesson here is that all souls or atmas are one and the same. That Baba is in, and was in all. In *Shri Sai Satcharita*, Chapter 9, Mrs. Tarkhad feeds a dog, then a mud smeared pig and Baba's hunger is appeased.

(ii) The Kolamba (Bowl)

Baba took *bhiksha* and mixed the food in the *kolamba*. He partook of it and gave it as prasad to the devotees. The tongue, which is rather small, has the ability to taste. After the food is gulped there is no taste. This small organ is responsible for all happenings. Baba had total control over His tongue. Whether the food was tasty, good or stale mattered little to Him. By taking bhiksha from Nandram, a Jain marwadi, he taught equality of vision that caste or creed mattered little. Thus we should treat food as Brahma and not hanker for tasty food. Life may shower both bitterness and sweetness. We should accept it with good grace as prasad given by Baba. Baba took *bhiksha* from five houses instead of seven houses as is followed in the Madhukari system [*parampara*] of Datta Bhaktas. The word 'Madhukari' comes from the act of bees collecting honey, they flit from flower to flower collecting nectar and store it.

So by taking Madhukari from seven houses, one learns the valuable lesson of not hoarding our possessions only to leave it behind upon death. Whatever is given as bhiksha is eaten with reverence and that amount should satisfy hunger.

The possible symbolism of the seven houses is related to the seven appetites, that is – the five senses, the mind and the intellect.

Surya [the Sun God] rides on a chariot driven by seven horses, or the five senses and the Ego complex. The Sun is the life giver and the whole world is dependent on it. Baba by begging showed that He does not care for the Body complex.

41

The *five* houses symbolise the five *pranas*. Which are 1. *Prana* or the vital forces that receive everything into the body, 2. *Aapana* which excretes what is not required, 3. *Samana* which receives all that is brought by pranas and assimilates it, 4. *Vyana,* the circulatory system that carries assimilated food to the different parts of the body, 5. *Udayana* which protects and serves as a body guard to the individuality and the ego helping it to lift the thoughts to new heights of better understanding.

Baba lead a life of fakiri [poverty]. It was a simple life. His needs were few. Baba's attire states that philosophy and His kafni reflected this. His kafni though torn and tattered was clean and 'snow white'. The kafni is symbolic of *maya*. Maya functions through two powers known as *avarna* [covering] and *viksepa* [projecting] *kashya* or white dress represent the state of having burnt all desires. If they are smoldering in cinder form they wear yellow. If they have reached beyond that they wear white a symbol of purity and flawlessness. So one learns that we are covered and mired in Maya, which should be torn apart and uncovered.

Baba's kafni was made of a coarse [*manjarpat*] cloth. In the early days Baba used to wear either an orange or white kafni. Then Bala Shimpi stitched a green kafni for Him. Baba asked Bala to make only white kafnis for Him. In the Dwarkamai there would be bundles of kafnis lying in the corner. Baba would not wear a new kafni easily. Often Baba could be seen sitting in the Sanctum Sanctorum and stitching the torn kafni. Tatya would pester Him to change into a new kafni. But Baba would put it off saying He would do so the next day. Thus days would pass by. Tatya would insert his finger into the tear and widen it. So Baba was forced to wear a new kafni. Sometimes Baba would distribute kafnis. Baba would give His kafnis to some of His devotees. They were Balaram Mankar, Udavesh Bua, Kaka Dixit, Tatya Sahib Nulkar, just to mention a few.

On one of Nulkar's visit to Shirdi he writes – "In the afternoon Appa Kote came and stood near the pillar of the Chavadi. He was twisting a rag around his fingers I asked him if his finger was hurt? He said, "No" and told me that the rag was a piece from Baba's kafni. I asked him why he tore it? He said Baba tears the kafni for wicks and this bit was hanging out .So I took it. I prayed to be given the piece and he gladly gave it." Little did Tatya Sahib know that Baba would Himself give him His kafni? One afternoon Baba summoned Tatya Sahib to the Dwarkamai. Tatya Sahib of course went immediately. Baba took off His kafni and gave it to him saying, "Take this it will keep you warm on cold winter nights".

Here a Leela of Baba's kafni is appropriate. Jyotindra Tarkhad was devoted to Baba from a very young age. Their relationship was more than a father and son. On one of his visits to Shirdi this wonderful incident took place. Jyotindra Tarkhad (photo 55) was ever willing to do Baba's seva, without expecting any returns. One day Baba told Jyotindra that He was going to Lendi Baugh to bathe. He asked him whether he would do a chore for Him? Baba said, "Its not a difficult task, I will bathe. Before doing so I will hand you My kafni. Take it to the well and wash it. As you know I take an extremely long time to bathe, and it will dry in the meantime. But do not allow it to trail on the ground. So hold it up. Okay!" Jyotindra readily agreed.

But he instinctively felt that there was a lesson in this chore. Then Baba entered the room to have His bath. Jyotindra waited outside for Baba to hand over His kafni. After quite a long time he got impatient. He decided to peep through the slat in the door. What he saw left him speechless and spellbound. There was Baba and from each and every pore He was emanating light. The light was so powerful that he feared losing his sight. He at the same time was repentant for trying to see Baba in the nude. At that very moment Baba called out to him to take the kafni.

Hastily Jyotindra took the kafni. He went to the well and carefully washed, rinsed and wrung it. Then he stepped into the mid day sun and held the kafni with both hands above his head. As time passed by the kafni instead of getting lighter from drying started getting heavier and heavier. His arms ached as time went by and he knew he would fail. As a last resort he started praying to Lord Hanuman to give him strength to complete the chore "O! Hanuman destroyer of Lanka. Give me some of your strength so I can fulfill this seva. O! Hanuman bhakta of Rama help me to perform this service as a bhakta and sevak of Baba." His lips moved silently in prayer. Just then Baba yelled "Arre Bhau why are you praying to Hanuman for help." At that very moment the kafni started getting lighter. Needless to say Jyotindra confessed to Baba and begged for forgiveness. Baba always carried His *satka* [danda] with Him The *satka* is symbolic of *dehadand* or discipline, the tumeral or *Kamandulu* symbolises compassion to all living beings and kaupin [Head dress] is symbolic of sacrifice.

(iii) The Horse Shyam Karan

I have often wondered why 'A Fakir would need a horse?' The word 'ashwa' has many meanings. Ashwa means 'The great eater' so one can possibly say that the horse represents the destruction or eating away of our 'karmas'. Ashwa also means infinite knowledge. This knowledge could help in dispelling the love for transient materialistic things, thus ending the lure for the temporary and worldly things. Helping one on the journey from the unreal to the real.

Lord Indra represents ego and he rides a horse. [Ref *Nirukti*] The Bhadrinayka Upanishad, Chapter 1, *ovi* 5 describes the symbology of the Horse as follows:

The head of the sacrificial horse is the dawn, its eyes the sun, its the vital force the air, its open mouth the fire called vaisvanara and the body is the year. Its back is heaven, its belly the sky, its hoof the earth, its sides the four quarters [time of day]. Its ribs the intermediate quarter, its members or genitals the seasons; its joints the months and the fortnight. Its feet the days and night, its bones the stars and the flesh the clouds. Its half digested food the sands, its blood vessels the rivers. Its liver and spleen the mountains; the hairs the herbs and trees. Its foreparts the ascending sun, its yawning the lightening, its shaking of the body thunder, it's making water the rain and its neighing is voice.

The word 'Shyam' literally means a flawless, pleasing black. But the word in Hindu mythology could mean pure and holy. It has been prefixed to other words to convey different meanings. For example, Shyam Sunder is used to refer to Shri Krishna, Shyam Kant or Shri Shankar.

Shyam Karan was the name of the horse or ashwa of the Ashwamedha. The *rinanubandh* between Baba and Shyam Karan was deep and unfathomable. At every aarti he danced with joy and after the aarti was the first to bow to Baba. Baba then applied udi to his forehead and then gave the rest of the bhaktas udi. The horse that symbolises the whole cosmos bows before Baba and dances with joy when Baba is worshipped. Little wonder that his samadhi is in Lendi Baugh. After Baba's Mahasamadhi the horse would dance in the Samadhi Mandir at every aarti. This he did till his death. The horse took Mahasamadhi in 1945 and his samadhi lies in Lendi Baugh.

(iv) Khadaws [Sanyasi's Wooden Footwear]
Baba walked about in Shirdi bare foot thus sanctifying the soil by walking on it. But He did give *khadaws* to a few devotees. All materialistic things like *kanchan* (gold or wealth), *kamini* (women and vice), *bhumi* (land and property) should be stamped out of the mind by these wooden *khadaw* (wood represents the earth).

Kaka Dixit was fortunate to receive khadaws from Baba. At that period of his life he had already attained an ascetic frame of mind. Baba made him stay in solitude on the top floor of his Wada where he meditated and studied various religious books. Thus Baba confirmed His approval by giving him khadaws (photo 43).

Nana Sahib Nimonkar was another fortunate devotee. He and his wife came to reside in Shirdi and from morning to night they spent their time doing Baba's seva. Baba looked after their spiritual welfare. He wished to read the Bhagwad Gita, which was in Sanskrit, a language he did not know. Baba reading his thought said, "Why don't you read the Pothi?" Nana replied that he did not know Sanskrit. Baba immediately said "Never mind. Masjid Aayi will teach you. Begin today". He took Baba's advice and soon became so proficient that he could hold discourses. Then he read the *Gita* and the *Dnyaneshwari*. Nana Sahib took samadhi [died] two months after Baba's Mahasamadhi. During that time he had intense 'Dhyasa' [absorption] in Baba. He was a Ram Bhakta and he died saying 'Sri Ram'. It was very appropriate for him to receive khadaws from Baba. These khadaws he did not wear, but venerated them as a gift from Baba. They are kept in his prayer room in his home in Nimon Gaon.

Things Given to Kaka Dixit [Hari Sita Ram Dixit]
Kaka Dixit whose very name proclaims a devotee par excellence was highly educated and was a solicitor in Bombay with many political laurels, he was socially and economically well off. He was forty-five years old in 1909, when he came to Shirdi at Chandorkar's advice. Since then he had only one thought and that was to be with his Guru. Much to the dismay of friends and admirers, he closed his lucrative practice in 1912 and made Shirdi his home. It was on Ram Navami 1911 that Dixit had his *Griha Pravesh* (entering the newly built home with due rituals and puja) and started living in Dixit wada (*Shri Sai Satcharita,* Chapter 4).

From 1912 he spent his time in solitude reading the various books prescribed by Baba for nine months. Thus he progressed spiritually by leaps and bounds. Baba took care of his spiritual progress. Along the way he gave him gifts that Dixit cherished.

1. Kafni
The word Kafni probably comes from the word *Kafan* – meaning shroud. It symbolises sacrifice. Baba gave Dixit His Kafni when he was spiritually ripe. Baba also allowed him (Dixit) to dine with him in Dwarkamai. Dining with his guru besides being a honour, removes the feelings of caste, creed and superiority. Kaka would wear this Kafni and would perform his worship and meditation.

2. Khadaws

3. Baba's portrait

4. Silver khadaws or padukas (photo 44) in a box with Maruti's image on its lid. Baba asked Kaka to carry this box with him wherever he went, as it would protect him.

Krishna Kashinath Khajgewale alias Nana Sahib
Krishnanji (Nana Sahib) was born in Karala in Ratnagiri District. He was a Brahmin of Limaye family. His ancestors migrated from the coast of Maharashtra. His forefathers were brave men and well built. Jwaji Pant alias Anna Khajgewale enroute to the mainland carried with him only two sets of clothes and food. On the way he was blessed with a vision of Jothiba (a deity). The blessing of Jothiba enabled him to procure a job of Khajgewale (Manager) in the Peshwa dynasty. Hence the title of Khajgewale was conferred on him. With the title came affluence and power and his family lived well.

Nana Sahib was born in the Khajgewale family, at the time when the British annexed the Peshwas. Some of the elders joined the British Government, but Nana's father refrained from doing so. This resulted in the loss of the title and poverty set in.

They had ancestral wadas and were overseers of Shingwe gaon in Nasik. Along with the loss of the title they lost everything.

Sudakar, Nana's grandson says, "Disheartened Nana Sahib wandered about here and there. Then in Niphard, he met

Nana Sahib Bharve who took him to Shirdi". In Shirdi Nana Sahib found peace and decided to make Shirdi his home. Soon he became the trainer of Shyam Karan, Baba's beloved horse (photo 72).

Nana Sahib was well built and a good wrestler. But most of all he loved horses and had good knowledge of them. It was in 1910 or 1912 that he arrived in Shirdi. Seeing him Baba said, "Seven generations of yours had Lakshmi (wealth) and now she has left for some time. But will return again after a while". Indeed at present the family is affluent.

The *Khajgewales* were responsible for starting the "Ganapathi" festival in Shirdi. Nana Sahib loved to listen to Das Ganu's kirtan and his faith in Baba increased by leaps and bounds. He and his father Bahu Sahib would often give Baba a session of *malish* (massage).

When Shyam Karan died his samadhi was made in the Lendi Baugh. There was a board in front of the Samadhi saying, "Shrimanth Sardar Nana Sahib Khajgewale was the trainer of Shyam Karan, who taught him to bow to Shri Sai Baba. This is the Samadhi of this fortunate horse". (Ref. Santkavi Shri Darshan Ganu Maharaj Darshan).

Now the Khajgewales' are residing in Pune.

Khalbatta (Pestle and Mortar)

"Ghavune Kesar Cha Vati, mage lavethi hasthe uti tambula Arpithe kara se Punti Prasanna Drsti Sai Che." Dabolkar writes this loving ovi (couplet) [*Shri Sai Satcharita*, Chapter 37, Ovi 191].

Taking the small bowl (usually a silver bowl) full of saffron, he would apply the paste on Baba's Divine hands. Then offer tambul in his palm. During this puja ritual Baba's expression would be divinely pleasing." This was part of the ritualistic puja offered by Bapu Sahib Jog at the Chavadi. Following the Chavadi procession, from the Dwarkamai to Chavadi every alternate day.

"Treyo Dashgune" Veeda or Tambul
1. Shira Kadlele Paan (Divine Beetle Leaf), 2. Phodleli Supari (Brokened arecanut), 3. Chuna (Lime), 4. Kairacha kath (Resin from the kher tree), 5. Kesar, (saffron), 6. Kasturi (sweet smelling resin), 7. Badam (almond), 8. Jaist Madhue (sweetening spice), 9. Jaipathri (bay leaf),10. Valchi (cardamom), 11. Lavang (Clove), 12. Jaiphal (nutmeg), 13. Suvarn (gold)

These thirteen ingredients are pounded together. A fairly fine powder is procured and then offered to Baba. No ritualistic puja is complete to the Sadguru without offering Tambul or "Paanvida" and "Dakshina". During Baba's sojourn in Shirdi this "Khalbatta" was used for that purpose. After Baba's Mahasamadhi in 1918, Tatya Kote Patil kept the khalbatta (photo 74) with him. He then gave it to Dadaji Gopinath Joshi.

Leela 15:   Hazarat Durvesh Haji Mohamed Siddique Phalke

In the eleventh chapter of the *Shri Sai Satcharita*, the incident of Baba's wrath on Siddique Phalke (photo 42) is given. How Baba put forth three questions to him. And the wonderful answers that Siddique Phalke gave. Durvesh Haji Mohamed Siddique Phalke was born in Kalyan around 1841. He was an affluent jamindar [land owner] and had vast acres of farmlands. He was sophisticated, intelligent, well read and spiritual. He had travelled widely. Baghdad, Constantinople, Mecca were but some of the places that he had visited. Dada Sahib Khaparde has recorded one of his visits to Shirdi dated 14-12-1911 to 23-12-1911 in his *Shirdi Diary*.

Dada Sahib Khaparde who was himself extremely learned and spiritual, states that Siddique Phalke was a gentleman of the 'old sort', a Karma-Margi and very intelligent. He was spiritually developed and learned. The conversations that they had were pleasant and instructive. Baba liked Phalke a great deal and is said to have granted his wish.

During that visit Phalke had a vision and he asked Dada Sahib to ask Baba its meaning. The vision was about three girls and a blind woman who had come to amuse him. He ordered them to go out or they would be kicked out and began to pray. The three girls and that blind woman fled upon hearing the prayer. He then blessed everyone in the room; and in the house and the whole village. Dada Sahib was barely seated before Baba when Baba said, "He was beaten last night by something on His private parts and hands. He then applied oil; wandered about, had a stool, sat near the fire and felt better."

Siddique Phalke was married to Kursheed and had two sons named Gulam Mustafa and Mohmed Mukram. Phalke loved to wear spotlessly white clothes. Whenever the Dwarkamai was washed with cowdung, Baba would summon Phalke and make him sit on the wet floor much to Phalke's discontent. But when he got up his clothes remained spotless as before.

Baba loved and had great respect for Phalke and whenever permission was granted for his departure Baba would walk the hundred paces with him and see him off at the breach in the wall. Phalke lived in a huge building in Kalyan called Phalke wada and it is still there even today.

In chapter 11 of *Shri Sai Satcharita* the story of Siddique Phalke's attempt to obtain Baba's grace is given. Phalke stays for nine months in the north facing Chavadi, trying in vain to enter the Sanctum Sanctorum. Then he seeks Shama's help, and Baba finally relents. Then Baba asks Shama to ask Phalke whether he will carefully walk the straight and narrow path that goes beyond the 'Baravi well'. Siddique Phalke answers that whatever difficulty he may encounter he will carefully tread that path.

In fact, there is no well called 'Baravi' in Shirdi or the neighbouring villages. Baba possibly uses the word barvi to mean twelve. Here Baba asks Siddique Phalke whether he is willing to tread the straight and narrow path [The Spiritual Path] fraught with difficulties. Whether he is willing to do a twelve year penance [tapasya]? The penance of the twelve inner disciplines, which are as follows: 1. Viveka [discrimination], 2. Vairagya [renunciation], 3. Niswartha [selflessness], 4. Sama [calmness], 5. Dama [self-control], 6. Uparati [self-withdrawal], 7. Titiksha [forbearance], 8. Samadhana [self-settled], 9. Shradha [faith], 10. Satsang [holy-company], 11. Maun [silence of the mind], 12. Ekanta-Dhyana [solitude and meditation]. Lastly the Guru's grace without which nothing is possible.

Siddique Phalke indeed came to Baba of and on for twelve years. The next question was "Will you give Me 40,000 Rs in 4 installments?" To which Siddique Phalke answers, "I will gladly give 40,00000 [forty lakhs] if asked. What then of thousands? Only let me be at His feet." Siddique Phalke was affluent but was he willing to part with his money. The deeper meaning could be given as follows. The four installments could mean *manas* (mind), *budhi* (intelligence), *aham* (pride), *chitta* (consciousness).

Through Antharkarnya Chatustaya, the zeros could represent the three bodies – Bhautik or physical, Shukshma or subtle, Kaaran or casual [This is the first zero].

The 2nd zero could be Triputi that is Jnana [knowledge] 2 jneya [experience of knowledge] and jnathru [the person who experiences it].

The 3rd zero could be the panch indriyias that consist of 5 *kamindryas*, which are touch, taste, smell, sight and hearing. And five *jnanindriyas* that are *shabda* [ears], *sparsha* [skin], *rupa* [eyes], *rasa* [tongue] and *gandha* [smell].

51

The 4th zero implies the six Arishadvargas are kama, krodha, madha, matsaraya, moha, lobha. The Haji replies that he will give 40,00,000 [Forty lakhs] thus there are 2 more zeros.

Therefore the 5th zero could imply that he is willing to give five '*Pranas*' that are *prana, apana, udana, vyana*, and *samana*. The 6th zero could mean the five Koshas. That are *annamaya kosha, pranamaya kosha, monomaya kosha vignamaya kosha* and *annandamaya kosha*. Here the Haji seems prepared to surrender in toto that is *Sampurna Sharanagathi*. Baba then gets angry and throws the vessels when He hears that the Haji is ready to give 40,00,000. Baba knows that the sishya is ready for total surrender. The guru wants the sishya to be purified without having a tinge of Prarabdha so He burns it by showing anger. Then he takes 55 rupees from His pocket, and counting them, one by one He places them in Phalke's hands. Money is Shri. The 5+5 symbolically could be the dress code of the sanyasi – 1) *Sirvesh* or *Kaupin* signifies total surrender, 2) *Pitambar* signifies sacrifice, 3) *Danda* that is *Deha Dand* or discipline, 4) *Kamandalu* stands for compassion and 5) *Khadaw*. Then He bought a basket of mangoes and presented it to him. And he was accepted in Baba's durbar. Mangoes represent auspiciousness.

The 3rd question that Baba asks is – "What part of the sacrificial goat would he like to eat? Does he want to eat the meat covered bones or is his heart set on eating the sex organs?" Baba wants to make sure that he has no Ashwath of any kind left. Be it for delectable food or sensual appetite. Siddique Phalke's answer is incredible. He states that if Baba wishes to give him anything he would cherish a crumb from the Kolambah.

Meaning of 55
Sadguru Sai Baba gave Rs 55 to Phalke, by which He may have conveyed the transient nature of this world or sansara. On the other hand, He may have conveyed the *sara* or gist of the Vedas. Shri Krishna while giving Updesh to Arjuna from

the *Bhagwad Gita* says, "This world or universe is like the Ashwatha Vriksha. Whose roots are on the top, and branches are down. This Vriksha is everlasting. The Vedas are the leaves. One who knows this knows the Vedas." The entire Universe is compared to the Ashwatha Vriksha, although this tree does not yield any flowers or fruit, yet it is compared to the universe. Why? Because it represents and reflects all the characteristics of the universe, the body and life itself.

The very name "Ashwatha" indicates the transient existence of this worldly life. Every fraction of the second is not constant, and is changing. The word possibly comes from "Ashwa" or the horse. The horse is vivacious and restless by nature. If one adds all the digits from one to ten it is equal to fifty-five. The meaning of 'Ashwatha' is as follows :-

1. Moola Prakruthi of this Vriksha of the world is the Parabhrama or super natural power. The Ashwath tree has the two varieties of fruit —

    (a) Fruit of Eha or Pravithi Marga or Path of materialistic life.

    (b) Fruit of Par or Nivrithi Marg or path of spirituality and of self-realisation. The Ashwath tree was three branches of the roots or the three Gunas, namely – Satva, Rajas, and Tamas.

2. Four varieties of taste in the two fruits namely Dharma, Aartha, Kama, and Moksha.

3. Five branches of the roots from the top to bottom namely- Shabdha, Sparsha, Roopa, Rasa, and Gandha.

4. Sub branches of the ariel roots or the six stages of the life cycle that is the Bhava Vikras – namely
    a) The foetal stage
    b) Taking birth
    c) Growing
    d) Maturing [from infancy to Youvanavastha]
    e) Deterioration

53

f) Finally Death

5. Seven layers of the bark of the tree. These represent the tissues that make the body. Namely the colour of the skin, and the skin itself, the muscles, blood in the blood vessels, the bone marrow, fat and adipose tissue and the skeletal system.

6. The eight branches and twigs [Non-ariel]

   a) Gods and Goddess

   b) Gandarvas

   c) Manavas

   d) Danvas

   e) Rakshasas

   f) Paishas

   g) Animals and birds

   h) Trees, plants and creepers

   i) The nine holes of the tree represent the orifices of the body.

   j) Ten leaves comprising of 5 Jnanindriyas and 5 Karmendriyas.

Leela 16: Neelkant Ramachandra Sahasrabudhe alias Baba Sahib

Neelkant and Tatya Sahib Nulkar were friends right from school as both were classmates at Poona High School in Pune. Then time and destiny made them go separate ways. Nulkar went to Pandarpur and he lost touch with Neelkant.

Neelkant (photo 61) was kind, caring and a very spiritual person. He had studied the Vedas and the Upanishads and practised their teachings. At every opportunity he had satsung with *Gyanies* and *satpurashas* and gained spiritual knowledge from them. As a social reformer he was at the forefront for woman's rights and issues like education for women and remarriage of child widows. In fact, where ever and whenever the need arose to help the down trodden he participated with zeal. During the plague epidemic of 1904 he invested his time, energy and money in caring for the patients. Since most of the residents had fled, he carried the dead to the funeral grounds himself.

He did many jobs. He worked as a military accountant, secretary of the Municipal Corporation at Bombay and even as a manager for the Bhosle family. Once a friend asked him about the importance of a guru! He answered that a guru cannot be got from the bazaar. The sadhak should be full of kindness, humility, having conquered the six internal enemies, should be patient and then the guru himself will shower his grace on him.

In 1911, Nana Sahib Chandorkar wanted to send some cooking utensils to Shirdi. He was looking for a suitable person for this chore. By chance he happened to meet Neelkant and asked him to do so. Neelkant pleaded lack of funds. So Nana made all the necessary arrangements and sent him to Shirdi. He went to Sathe Wada and to his surprise saw Nulkar seated there. Though Nulkar did not recognise him, Neelkant happily called out to him. Nulkar being the perfect host invited him to be his guest. At first when Nulkar and the other devotees were listening to satsung, and trying to decipher what Baba said, Neelkant thought they needed to be in a mental asylum.

When he went for darshan Baba said, "By doing Namaskar to Tatya Sahib and Bapu Sahib Jog does not detract you from your character, and you lose nothing". Then Baba added, "Keep doing Tatya Sahib's seva". Baba repeated this command for three consecutive days.

Shama time and again requested permission for Neelkant's departure. At first Baba said, "Let him go after four or five days". When Shama asked for permission after some days Baba said, "Let him lie like a dog in front of the Masjid. He has to undertake some important task." So Neelkant decided to stay on. Of and on he teased Tatya Sahib saying, "According to the wish of your guru, tell me what seva I can do for you?" Tatya Sahib of course knew that there was a deeper meaning and only time would tell that.

During his stay Neelkant got many wonderful experiences and soon realised that Baba was an *antaryami*. When Neelkant had doubts Baba would send him to Bapu Sahib Jog or Kaka Sahib Dixit on the pretext of getting dakshina. There they would read the pothi and the very verse or chapter would give him the answer. Thus his devotion to Baba increased by leaps and bounds. Meanwhile Tatya Sahib started showing signs of diabetes. The disease was uncontrollable, as time went on. Tatya Sahib developed carbuncles that spread at an alarming rate. Neelkant was constantly at Tatya's side nursing him, and helping with the dressing of the wounds. As Tatya was unable to get out of bed, Neelkant would fetch water and help him to drink and to pass urine also. Tatya was overwhelmed and at the same time upset by this. Neelkant on the other hand did not think he was doing anything unusual. He remained with Tatya till his samadhi [death] nursing him and taking care of his every need.

Leela 17: **Lakshman Krishnaji Nulkar**
alias Tatya Sahib Nulkar

"A star has fallen behind the Masjid," said Baba when Tatya Sahib died. This speaks volumes of love and respect that Baba had for this great devotee. Baba lovingly called him "Tatyaba' or 'Mathara'. Tatya Sahib had the habit of writing about his visits to Shirdi to Nana Sahib Chandorkar. From these letters it is very evident that there was a the deep rinanubandh that existed between Baba and him. Tatya Sahib hailed from Jalgaon. He studied in Pune, worked in Pandarpur, retired and spent the last years of his life at Baba's feet in Shirdi.

In one of his letter to Nana Sahib he wrote, "On Friday I went to Dwarkamai. Baba was sitting with Amirbhai. Sai was smoking the 'chilum'. He said, "Hey desi tambako kadu laagthe" [This indigenous tobacco is bitter]. I had recently got an excellent Egyptian tobacco for my pipe and had thought would Sai accept some of it. So I said I'd fetch some for Him. Sri opened it, saw it and praised it. Amirbhai hastily filled the 'chillum'.

"Then Sri took a few puffs and returned the tin saying, 'It will be useful for Mahatara. The indigenous tobacco is good for us.' That very day Tatya Sahib proposed to get some mango juice made for Baba's *naivedya* from the delectable mangoes from Bombay. But only a few mangoes were left. I was praying that there would be mangoes coming for sale. Shortly thereafter Shyama came and said, "Baba said, 'Hey bhag Shyama Shambar ambe ghavya aani pushkal raas kadave aani khub khaava'

[Look here Shyama a hundred mangoes should be taken and plenty of juice prepared and eaten to full satisfaction]. In a few minutes a man with a basket of mangoes came along. I bought them and had plenty of juice. That Sunday I thought our mangoes were over. But wished and hoped that in the straw one stray mango would be found to send with the naivedya. I asked my wife and she said that at the bottom were four good ones and four rotten ones. So I took out two of the best ones to be kept in the naivedya dish. Within two minutes Appa Kote came and said that Baba wanted two mangoes. You can imagine how glad I was, I told Appa to bring back one slice from Baba's left over. But he forgot. Baba cut one mango and ate it. Then He cut slices from the second one; gave some slices to Shyama and others. Taking the last slice He said "Aapan sagale khatho thya Matharala ekh phank nako kare Shyama [We are eating the mangoes! Shouldn't that old man get at least one slice Give this one to him].

"Then Appa remembered my message. On another visit Tatya Sahib took shira as offering and Baba accepted it. A basket of mangoes were placed before Him. He said, "Mahatara la aasu dey kahi udhya khaaeyel 'kahi parva khaaeyel'" [Keep it for Mahatara. He can eat some tomorrow and some the day after]. So the basket was put away. When Sri went to the new Chavadi where we were going to stay, he said, "Stay at the Wada [Sahib's Daramshala]. He actually took us there. There horses were tied. The kitchen was just being completed and a lot of mud and debris was lying around. Sri said, "This is a nice snug and protected place. Do you like it?" I said yes we would stay here. Then we came out when Sai said, "No don't stay here stay in the new Chavadi! Tomorrow if you like you may go to the Wada". We had reached the new Chavadi and Sri had almost reached the masjid. When He whispered in Tatya Sahib's ear, "Its damp in the Wada so stay in the Chavadi". This letter shows how much Baba cared for Tatya Sahib's comfort.

Raghunath of Dopeshwar alias Kaka Puranik

After taking Baba's darshan Tatya Sahib (Lakshman Krishnaji Nulkar) was a changed man. He made Shirdi his home and breathed his last there. Baba lovingly called him "Mahatara" [old man] not because of his age. For he was only forty-eight years old, when he took Samadhi [died]. But because he was an "Old Soul" [highly developed and evolved soul]. When he found his Sadguru, he was mature and ripe enough for Baba to give him "Sadgati". Besides sadgati, Baba also gave him many earthly gifts like Lakshmi (money). His kafni [Fakir's shroud or garment] and two photographs of Himself. This photograph was housed at his Jalgaon Home. His grandson Raghnuath Vishwanath Nulkar (photo 21) was concerned that "Baba in that photograph was not being tended to appropriately", so he brought the photograph to Pune and after ritualistic puja, bhajan and annadan gifted it to Sai parivar.

This Maha Satpurush was Baba's contemporary [1821-1910] He was from Rajapur jilha in the Ratnagiri district. Tatya Sahib Nulkar and DR Pandit were devoted to him. Once Tatya Sahib's 6-months-old nephew was sick at Jalgaon, and Kaka Puranik sent *angara* [vibhuti] to be given to the child. And the hopelessly ill child recovered. Tatya Sahib writes to Chandorkar saying, "At Phandarpur when Kaka Puranik (photo 28) was there in Feb [1909] he had given me 4 Rs saying, 'Keep them'. I connected this with the story 'Thyane maje char bhau maarle' [He killed my four brothers] .You remember at Easter in Shirdi we were asked to come down with Rs 4 each by Shri Sai Baba. I connected all this. The number 4 indicates the ego complex, i.e. *manas* [mind], *budhi* [intelligence], *chitta* [consciousness], and *ahankar* [pride]. And the need to surrender them at the feet of the guru. And to kill the four components [brothers] that leads a devotee astray."

In his insightful letter he describes how both the Gurus worked in unison on the same subject. Thus strengthening and affirming the faith of the devotee.

Dr Jaganath Uithal Pandit Geminis

Dr Pandit was related to Tatya Sahib Nulkar on his mother's side. He was devoted to Kaka Puranik. In *Shri Sai Satcharita*, 11 the story of Dr Pandit is beautifully described where he offers guru puja to Baba by marking His forehead with a Tripunda of sandal wood paste. As this was the puja he offered to his guru Kaka Puranik. Pandit was devout and innocent. His action conveys the highest truth that there is no difference between his Brahmin guru and the Kafni-clad Sai Baba. And Baba perceiving his clear conscience was quite pleased rather than flying into a rage.

Dr Pandit (photo 27) hailed from Kolapur [Ratnagiri district] and was a medical doctor. He studied in a medical college in Calcutta. His descendents are living in Pune. The Tripunda is symbolic of the gunas [Raja, Tama, Satva] of which this universe is made of. When Dr Pandit drew the Tripunda on his Guru's forehead he believed that his guru could destroy these gunas. Befittingly he drew the Tripunda on 'Triputi Nashak' Baba, who could easily destroy these gunas.

Leela 18: Viswanath Lakshman Nulkar

Baba's grace enveloped Viswanath (photo 21) right from birth, as he was born to the blessed Lakshman and Janki Nulkar. He was born on 9th November 1889 in Narsingpur, Madhya Pradesh. He was the younger son of Tatya Sahib. His primary education was at New English School, Pune. He then studied in the Deccan College of Commerce, Pune. Later he worked for the Municipal Corporation. He first visited Shirdi with Tatya Sahib in 1909. Vishu as his parents called him was asked by Baba to go immediately to the 'Shala' [school], which was the residence of Radha Krishna Mai. It was steeped in spirituality. He then returned home with his parents. Though he joined college his heart was at Shirdi and he started contemplating on vairagya. He had an intense desire to go and stay with Baba and do seva there. He was fortunate enough to do so. Tatya was anxious as Vishu wanted to become a sanyasi and had left home. So he went to see how he was doing? He was rather surprised to see a young ascetic, dressed like Baba on the banks of the River Godavari only to find that he was Vishu. Baba understood the turmoil that Tatya and his family were in and after a few months He sent him home. Vishu did complete his education and worked for the Municipal Corporation.

In 1914, he married Susheela Jemenis the niece of S.V Jemenis. The bride was chosen by Baba. Tatya Sahib took two photographs of the prospective brides to Baba for approval. Baba put His finger on Susheela's photograph. They were blessed with six children and lived in Pune where Vishnu worked. He took samadhi in Satara.

Baba lovingly called him 'Gipra' [the long haired one]. His younger brother Waman Rao was born in 1892 in Narsingpur. He studied in the same school as his brother. After successfully completing his medical degree he became a general practitioner.

Leela 19: **Maina Tai Ganesh Kuvelkar**
[Chandorkar's daughter]

She was the daughter of Nana Sahib and Radhabai Chandorkar born in 1887. She first visited Shirdi in 1900 when she was thirteen-years-old along with her family. They visited Shirdi numerous times and Maina Tai was able to witness many a Leelas, and hear the advice given to her father. She learnt early in life the consequences of disobeying Baba's orders at the time of departure. Once she and her family were going to Nasik to attend a marriage. Baba didn't give them permission to go, they left nonetheless. The result was they were hungry for three to four hours. On the other hand obeying Baba's orders, no matter how exasperating it may sound, was sure to give a comfortable, successful and safe journey.

She was married at a very young age, and moved to Pune with her husband. But he died in the plague epidemic of 1904. When she became pregnant her mother took her to Jamner. At the time of delivery she had a great deal of difficulty. It was that time when 'The Jamner Miracle' took place. [*Shri Sai Satcharita*, chapter 33]. The compassionate Baba sent Udi and Adkar's aarti through Ramghir Bua. On the way Baba appeared as a peon and took Ramghir by tonga to Jamner and disappeared.

At Nana's home, Navchandi Havan and Saptashati Path was recited to overcome the difficult labour. It was only when Baba's udi dissolved in water touched Maina Tai's lips that the pain subsided. She had a safe delivery. The child however died and this made Maina Tai very dejected. Das Ganu on hearing the tragic circumstance, gave a pair of Baba's silver padukas and comforted her. She found solace therein. She lived with her in-laws in a large joint family and had a peaceful life. She died in 1945 in Pune.

Leela 20: **Bappaji Lakshman Ratna Parke**

His forefathers were experts in evaluating precious stones and diamonds for the Peshwas, hence the surname Ratna Parke. They were Brahmins and pujaris by profession. They migrated to Shirdi and made it their home. Bappaji (photo 17) was born in Shirdi to Lakshman and Yamuna Ratna Parke. In 1886, his father was the village priest and astrologer.

Since Bappaji knew Baba from childhood he had free reign of the Dwarkamai. He would spend most of his time with Baba. Baba loved him deeply, and often they would be found playing together. He started doing Baba's seva from 1910. Bappaji went to the Marathi school and studied up to seventh standard. He was very proficient in indigenous medicines. He would treat the villagers for minor illnesses.

His father was a very orthodox Brahmin and rigid in his ways. Once when Bappaji was extremely sick and at death's door, his father ran to Baba for cure. Baba shouted violently using abusive language, a little later Baba went to Bappaji's home. He laid His hand of benediction on Bappaji's forehead and he was cured. This incident further strengthened his faith and devotion. Their family has been living in the same home where Baba gave *shakshatkar* and cured him. It is behind the Vitthal Mandir. They were related to Shama and they gave him fifty square feet of land on which his house stands.

Tatya Sahib Nulkar was seriously sick with diabetic carbuncles and could not go for Baba's darshan. He yearned to see Baba. That afternoon Bappaji went to Dwarkamai to sit and chat with Baba. A few kids were teasing Baba at that time. Just then a hawker passed by selling cloth. Bappaji looked at the beautiful pieces and asked Baba if he could buy one.

Baba said "yes". He bought a red brocade piece and tied it around his head. Baba playfully pinched his cheeks, so he took the cloth and placed it on Baba's head. Baba acted like a child and put it back on Bappaji's head. This went on for some time and wonder of wonders Tatya Sahib could see this beautiful scene from Sathe wada.

As an adolescent Bappaji would go and sit against the wall of Dwarkamai. Whenever Baba had *Handi Annadaan* he sat there waiting for prasad. He watched Baba cook *mitha chawal* [sweet rice] with His bare hands without a twinge of pain or trace of burns. At other times Baba would make sixteen padari poli [sixteen layered chapaties]. Then roast them on the dhuni.

On the days when Baba bathed, He would ask him to bring pots of hot and cold water. Then mixing it to the right temperature He bathed. Bappaji and Bayaji would take turns to scrub Baba's back with the bathing stone. He states that Baba wore Pitambar after His bath, and tied His kaupin so fast that they could not make out how He did it. Later He would change into His kafni.

He says that Baba would distribute about five hundred rupees daily. He used to give Bayaji ten rupees, from which he had to purchase wood for Dhuni Maa. Ramachandra Dada got fifteen rupees for sugarcane. Often Baba would say "Sab paise ke Bhai. Apna koi nahi" [Roughly Translated – "Everyone belongs to wealth, We belong to no one"].

On 19th May, 1917 Lokmanya Tilak and Khaparde came for Baba's darshan. That time Bappaji was with Baba. When Baba took Mahasamadhi on 15th October 1918, he was in Dwarkamai. Baba sent the anxious and concerned devotees home. But a few devotees stayed behind and Bappaji was one of them. His father Lakshman Maama did the *kakad aarti* the next day [*Shri Sai Satcharita* – Chapter 43].

Bappaji got married to Gita Bai and had children. After his father's demise he became the pujari of Vithal Mandir. He took samadhi in May 1987.

Leela 21: Anna Sahib Karindkar

This gem of a devotee was born in Dhanu Road Station in Shake 1772 [1851]. He died at the age of eighty one on 24th March, 1931 at 2:30 a.m in Malyan. He was conscious till the end. He seemed to know that his end was near. He summoned his entire family and asked them to perform Baba's *aarti* and *naam jap*. His last wish was to hear the *Shrimad Bhagwad Gita* and it was read to him.

Anna Sahib studied up to seventh standard in the Marathi medium and discontinued because his eyes hurt terribly. But his love for reading only seemed to increase. His home had a well-stocked library. It contained numerous books both religious and non-religious, magazines of every kind and of course the newspaper. A philanthropist, social worker, and educationist, he spent his life doing good for the community. Averse to doing a job and working for others he took up farming.

From the yields of the farm he often donated grains to the needy, to temples, and various agencies. He would also give grain for *annadaan* to people for various functions.

The Shirdi Sai Baba Sansthan and *Sai Leela Magazine* were his favourite projects. Ever since the first Sai Leela magazine was published he subscribed to it, and prevailed upon others to do the same. Needless to say, that he preserved each and every magazine datewise very carefully. Further, he advertised and made announcements of weddings, ceremonies and other occasions, thus paying for their publication. It made him happy, that by doing so the magazine got funds. Time and again he sent donations through Dev, a disciple of Baba to the Shirdi Sai Baba Sansthan. Like an accountant he would set money aside, and sent it to the Sansthan for every festival celebrated in Shirdi. He subscribed to the magazine for hundred rupees. He then sent hundred rupees for each of his sons. Shri Krishna Janardhan, Keshav Mahadev and Haribhau Karnik. Thus he got his sons to become members, perforce. Once he had gone to Nana Sahib Chandorkar's house, there he found Das Ganu's *Bhakta Leelamrit* and *Sant Leelamrit* lying about uncared for. After taking permission from Nana Sahib, he sold them for one hundred and fifty rupees. He sent that money to Shirdi Sai Baba Sansthan, as a subscription for both of Nana's sons.

Baba's Grace enveloped him, and Baba came to his home through a photograph. The wonderful leela is given here. Keshav Ganesh Joshi was his son-in-law. Keshav got a portrait of Baba painted through the owner of Gyan Sagar Litho Press. He asked Kaka Sahib Mahajini for help, as Keshav liked the portrait that Kaka had and he wanted a similar one. Thus a beautiful portrait was painted. Then he got it framed with a rich coloured wood. When it was ready and he was satisfied, he and B V Dev took it home.

With due rituals it was hung on the wall. A few months later Dev visited Anna Sahib's home in Dhanu. He was very surprised to see that very same portrait in his home. Curious about this he asked Anna how that portrait came to his home. Anna said, "As you know that Joshi brought this portrait home, and hung it on the wall. A few days later he had a dream. Baba told him, "Take me to Dhanu, and give this portrait to Anna." Joshi had no choice, as it was Baba's wish." Needless to say that Anna performed morning and evening aarti daily. Chanted the *Vishnu Sahasranam*, offered Naivedya, and lovingly took care of it.

In 1910 Dev, Anna Sahib and Kavaji Patil visited Shirdi. They went to Dwarkamai and prostrated before Baba and sat down. Dev respectfully gave Baba dakshina of one rupee. Baba asked him for another rupee which he gladly gave. Then Baba put out His hand and asked for another rupee. Dev happily gave it. Thus He took three rupees from Dev.

Simultaneously Anna took out money for dakshina. Turning to Anna, Baba accepted the one rupee coin. Then He asked Anna for another rupee, which he humbly gave. Thus Baba took two rupees from Anna. From Kavaji He took nothing. Baba shouted at him, and would not allow him to enter the Sanctum Sanctorum.

On subsequent visits, much to Anna's discontent Baba did not ask Anna for dakshina. Though He did ask Dev. Upset with the turn of events, he asked Dev about this, "Why doesn't Baba ask me for dakshina? I'm more than willing to give Him Dakshina. Although I accompany you; He asks you, but not me?" Dev replied, "Baba gets other kinds of seva done through you. Dakshina is not the only seva one can do for Baba. And who can know why Baba does what He does. He is mysterious, and an enigma. However what He does will never harm us."

Leela 22: Sakharam Hari alias Bapu Sahib Jog

Baba loved him so much that when he first visited Shirdi, Baba would not allow him to return home and get his belongings. Bapu Sahib was probably born in 1856. He worked as a supervisor for the government and in 1909 he availed of the 'retiring furlough' and came to Shirdi with his wife. The couple had no children, and they lived comfortably on their pension.

One of Bapu Sahib close relative was the famous satpurush Vishnu Bua. Before visiting Shirdi he had visited Kabad to pay homage to Sadhu Sakharam Maharaj. He spent sometime there doing seva. Bapu Sahib thought that he would stay for a few days in Shirdi and then return to Kabad, and spend the rest of his life doing seva there. But Baba had other plans for him. At

Shirdi he stayed in Sathe wada. When the other devotees said something that he did not like he threatened to go to Kabad. Baba said, "Does the Wada belong to Sathe's father? I'll tell Dada Kelkar not to trouble you. You just stay peacefully there. Okay!" Baba spoke so sweetly that Bapu Sahib stayed on.

Bapu Sahib was a 'Chithpavan Konkansth Brahmin', orthodox, and strictly followed the 'Sovale' (State of purity) ritual. He was righteous, honest, and straightforward in his dealings. His wife was of a similar temperament and they were made for each other. Her name was Tai and Baba called her "Aayi". Bapu Sahib was a 'Datta Upasak' [staunch devotee and follower of the Datta ritual]. He silently went about doing his sadhana. The *devera* [shrine] in his room had all the gods. He would offer a kafni along with naivedya to Lord Datta on every Datta Jayanthi. One year while at Shirdi he had an irresistible desire to offer a kafni to Baba on Datta Jayanthi. So, he got Bala Shimpi to stitch a kafni. On Datta Jaanthi he took the kafni; and after doing puja to Baba offered the kafni. Baba accepted the Kafni, and in turn gave him one of His kafni as prasad. Happily he took the kafni and preserved it. In the evening he would wear the kafni, tie a white cloth around his head, and go for Baba's darshan. He called it "Durbari Poshak" [Court Dress]. At other times he wore ordinary clothes.

Bapu Sahib was kind-hearted and a thorough gentleman. But because of his position of power, and his dealings with the labour force he appeared stern. But he did have a quick temper. Baba, slowly but surely changed this. He lived frugally and had quite a bit of money saved. Baba knew that he was egoistic about his wealth. Baba kept demanding dakshina again and again from him till he was depleted of all his savings. Bapu Sahib learned a valuable lesson. His routine every month was to collect his pension from Kopergaon, pay his dues to the shopkeepers, and whatever remained he would place that before Baba. Baba trusted him immensely and would often give His money to him for safekeeping. Bapu Sahib would keep the money safely and was constantly aware that it was

Baba's money. When the need arose Baba would ask him to buy this or that from it. Baba would often give him hundred rupees, and a few days later jokingly say, "Bapu Sahib I gave you a hundred and twenty-five rupees a few days ago. Go and fetch it." Bapu Sahib would tell Baba that He had given him only hundred rupees. This happened quite a few times, and Bapu Sahib would indignantly say, "Baba I don't want to be involved with Your money transactions. Keep Your money with someone else." Baba would then pacify him saying, "Bapu Sahib don't get angry! I made a mistake, it was only a hundred rupees okay." Once a devotee gave Baba a guinea. Baba gave it to Bapu Sahib and said, "What is this?" He told Baba that it was a guinea or equivalent to fifteen rupees. Baba said, "It is worth thirty rupees you keep it and give Me thirty rupees".

Bapu Sahib looked after Baba's affairs, after Megha's (Baba's disciple) death on 19th January 1912. He was given the honour of performing Babas aarti till Baba's Niryan in 1918.

All the seva that Megha used to perform fell on Bapu Sahib's shoulders – like Baba's aarti in Dwarkamai, evening aarti in Sathe wada, aarti in Dixit wada, and Guru Paduka Sthan. Bapu Sahib took his duties very seriously. Usually there were a substantial number of devotees present for the aarti. However, if there were a few or none at all, it did not bother Jog, he conducted the aarti with devotion and zeal. Bapu Sahib and Tai led a life of austerity. They were up at the crack of dawn. After bathing in cold water, they performed 'puja' to their household deities, followed by religious rituals, and reading of the pothi. Then they would go to the Dwarkamai for Baba's darshan. Bapu Sahib stayed at Baba's side doing all the chores required. Tai went home, and prepared the prasad for the aarti, and looked after the innumerable guests that Baba sent.

Tai was the epitome of bhakti. She was intensely devoted to Baba. Her love for her 'Guru' was so passionate that after Baba's niryan she lost self-control. She wandered the streets of Shirdi aimlessly, as if searching for her Guru. She had a vacant look on her face, oblivious of her surroundings. So desolate was she that she died two months later.

Bapu Sahib was very orthodox and strict about his way of eating. He observed Ekadashi and other fasts. On such days he would not touch onions. Baba respected this and never forced him to eat with Him. In fact, Baba would make him go home for lunch, often with some other devotees. Whenever the devotees offered sweets and fruits to Baba he would hand the whole basket or box to him.

Once Bapu Sahib asked Baba, as to when He would give him Sanyas. Baba replied, "As soon as you are free from your worldly responsibilities." Thus Bapu Sahib was now free. He stayed on at Shirdi for a few years and looked after Baba's samadhi.

After Kaka Sahib Dixit's death the other devotees left Shirdi. Being quite alone Bapu Sahib decided to go to Sakori. There he wore a kafni, and took sanyas. His decision to go to Sakori is perplexing, as he and Upasani (Baba's disciple) never had a cordial relationship. Once he dragged Upasani and brought him to Dwarkamai. Then he proceeded to tell Baba about the disagreement and asked Baba to be the judge. Nevertheless at Sakori he attended to Upasani with the same devotion as he would to Baba. As he died a sanyasi his samadhi lies in front of the Upasani Ashram in Sakori.

[Ref: *Sai Leela*, Ank 13, Year 4, 1926]

Leela 23:   **Samadhi of Bapu Sahib**
at Sakori

Kaka Sahib Dixit took Samadhi on Ekadashi day [Ekadashi is the eleventh day of the waning moon]. The month was jesth, the Shake 1848 (1926). Six months later Bapu Sahib took samadhi.

It so happened that a devotee had a vivid dream. Where he saw a group of devotees seated before Baba. These devotees had their eyes open. Next to them sat Kaka Sahib Dixit but he had his eyes closed, as if in meditation. Next to him was a seat that was vacant. The devotee in his dream asked Baba why the seat next to Kaka was vacant? And why did Kaka have his eyes closed? Baba replied, "That Dixit was a new comer and the empty seat was reserved for another dear devotee who would follow six months later." Thus Baba forewarned Bapu Sahib Jog's death.

Leela 24:   **Pralad Ramachandra**
Muley Shastri

Somnath Shankar Deshpande, son of Nana Sahib Nimonkar says that when Baba walked on the wet muddy streets of Shirdi he clearly saw 'Matsya' [fish] and 'Dhanushya' [bow] markings on Baba's footprints [*Devotees Experiences,* pp. 178]

These were not just markings or lines, but an indication that Baba was an avatar.

It was to meet Butti that Somnath and Muley Shastri came to Shirdi. And Baba gave Muley Shastri a marvellous experience that changed his life. The leela of Muley Shastri (photo 18) is described in *Shri Sai Satcharita,* Chapter 12. Pralad was born around 1879. He was a learned man, proficient in palmistry and astrology. He hailed from Nasik and his ancestors were gifted vast acres of land [*Jagir*] near Vazapur. That was seven generations before Pralad.

Orthodox in his behaviour, Muley Shastri strictly adhered to the ritual of Sovale [After having bath and donning silk clothes one cannot touch anything or anybody as it would detract him from his sanctified state]. When he went to the Dwarkamai to meet Butti he went to the Sanctum Sanctorum and took Baba's darshan. He was astounded to see Baba's feet and the markings on His sole. His professional curiosity was aroused. He could not contain himself. He asked Baba to allow him to read His palm. Baba asked him to sit down. In *Shri Sai Satcharita,* Chapter 12, it is stated that the *dwaja vajra* [Thunder Bolt] and *ankush* [Goad] symbols were clearly seen on Baba's sole. Baba asked him to sit down and later placed four bananas on his outstretched hand. In His characteristic humorous fashion Baba told a devotee to bring 'Ochre' dye, as He would don a saffron robe.

Muley Shastri then returned to his room and after proper ritual sat for meditation and prayers. In the meantime Baba sent Butti to get dakshina from him. Perturbed and disgusted he came to Dwarkamai. Lo! His guru was seated there instead of Baba.   [*Ref:* Sai Satcharita, *Chapter 12*]

Muley Shastri was married to Venu Bai and he had a son and a daughter. However he was restless and wandered about hither and *thither.* He was affluent as the royalty would consult him about 'auspicious' dates and time to conduct business deals and paid him handsomely. He smoked a chillum, and was very rigid about rituals. Baba however changed all this and before he left Shirdi, Baba gave him a pothi – a hand written book much like the laws of Manu 'on how to conduct one's self regarding family life.' Unfortunately the first few pages are missing so one does not know the title or the author's name. This pothi is hand written by different people. Interestingly the book was tailor made for his lifestyle. It lays down rules and regulations as to how one should behave as a *grastha* [householder] and laws about the different stages of life including *sanyas*.

Later Muley Shastri settled down in Vazapur and lead a peaceful 'contented life'. His descendents still continue the family tradition of making horoscopes and astrologic predictions.

Leela 25: Adveyndra Saraswati alias Gholap Swami or Baba Swami

Shivram Bhat Golap (photo 19) resided in Sangamner along with his wife. His wife gave birth to three sons but unfortunately they died in infancy. Shivram then vowed to his ishtadev that if he had a son that survived, he would dedicate that child to him. In due course his wife gave birth to a boy. So when their son turned two he along with his wife walked from Sangamner to Tryambakeshwar with their two-year-old son who was named Dundiraj.

Right from infancy Dundiraj had a preference for quiet and solitude. His father however taught him palmistry and astrology. According to his father's wish he got married and had a son named Ramachandra. Dundiraj however roamed about here and there and was totally detached from his family. But his wife was a responsible lady. She saw to it that

Ramachandra was educated and later left him with Nathu Appa. Nathu Appa was well versed in palmistry, astrology, Vedas and the Hindu law. Under his tutelage Ramachandra gained a deep knowledge of all these. Because of his proficiency the royalty and the rich businessmen often consulted him. Thus he was affluent and quite famous and people flocked to him with their troubles.

Once Ramachandra was walking on the road with his students and well-wishers when his father Dundiraj saw him and realised that Ramachandra was very fond of wealth, name and fame. He called him aside and told him something [gave updesh]. After that meeting Ramachandra's father became his *parthmic* guru and slowly his attachment for materialistic things, name and fame disappeared.

At Tilbandeshwar temple he started doing Maha Rudra puja and Surya puja and Sandhya and Agni seva. Along with braminical duties he continued the practice of astrology and palmistry.

He wrote various religious books. Upon his father's insistence he got married and had a daughter and two sons. His wife died after sometime. Then he took up Agni seva and married twice. As both his wives died he gave up Agni seva and took sanyas. He was then known as Adveyndra, Saraswati alias Gholap Swami or Baba Swami.

Along with sanyas he started looking for a *shatshatkari* Mahapurush for his guru. Living in Nasik he met many sadhus and saints but none appealed to him. One day he got up at 3:30 a.m., bathed in the Godavari and did his rituals and puja, After having completed his *sadhana* he was electrified by the presence of a satpurush, who had a magnetic personality, whose lustrous eyes spoke of his self-realisation. Gholap at once went and prostrated before him .The satpurush spoke gently, "To give you the fruit of your Karmas I have come all the way from Akkalkot." Gholap instantly knew that this Avatric purush was his guru. And to confirm it he said, "You have come all the way from Akkalkot to give me refuge."

At the very sight of his guru his mind attained a profound calm and peace, his questions received their answers and he was overwhelmed with love and gratitude. He wished to invite the mahapurush to his ashram (hermitage) but at that very moment he disappeared.

Marvelling at the miracle he returned to the ashram after that he spent his time in solitude but there was one burning desire and that was to go to Akkalkot and meet his guru again. Soon thereafter he did make that trip and at that time Swami Samarth was lying on a cot in the garden. He immediately prostrated before him, his guru gently asked, "And when did you come from Nasik?" This confirmed that the guru had chosen him as a disciple and he was speechless. Gholap spent some very fruitful time in Akkalkot and he progressed spiritually very rapidly. Then he returned to Nasik and brought *padukas* of Swami Samarth with him. He worshipped them and did seva of Swami Samarth. In Shake 1809 {1887} ashad thirteenth he took samadhi [died]. His Samadhi is in Nasik along with the padukas (photo 20).

Leela 26: Gopal Rao Mukundrao Butti

It is only befitting to write about Gopal Rao Mukundrao Butti (photo 81) during the month of Ashwin as devotees around the world are celebrating Dusssera and Baba's Mahasamadhi, on Vijay Dashami. I humbly thank Butti for giving us [Baba's devotees] the Samadhi Mandir. Every time I go in or even pass by the Samadhi Mandir (photo 83), I thank him from the bottom of my heart. Unfortunately very little is written about this great devotee.

His ancestors lived in Bardi, Nagpur. Their surname was Gharzaale. Legend has it that Gopal Rao's grandfather was a shrewd, but kind businessman and worked for the Bhosale royal family. When Raghuji Raje Bhosale died, the British seized and annihilated their regime. Their enormous wealth, gold, precious stones, along with elephants, horses and bulls were then auctioned off at a pittance. Sadashiv bought a lot of the gold and gems and further enhanced the wealth that the family already owned. Thus he earned the name booty that in English stands for loot.

The family business was mainly money lending and banking. Though they were wealthy and business minded; they did a lot of philanthropic work. They were just and had cordial relations with the rich and the poor. Butti's father Mukundrao was very spiritual and religious. Their ishtadevta was Krishna and all the religious festivals were celebrated with a great deal of pomp and show. Mukundrao's Guru was Gajanan Maharaj of Shehgaon and the Maharaj often visited their home.

They were Charak Brahmins of the Shandilya Gothra. The annals [puranas] of Charak Brahmins have featured their family tree very prominently. Vivid descriptions of their philanthropic and social deeds are mentioned. They built dharamshalas, gowshalas, schools and dispensaries and gave monetary help to poets writers and pundits.

Gopal Rao was born in 1873 in Sita Bardi, Nagpur and was the youngest of the three brothers. His father had a great influence on him. At the tender age of fifteen or sixteen he would return from school and after washing his hands and feet would take darshan of Gajanan Maharaj. Thus Gopal Rao was very cultured, highly educated [he studied in Manchester U.K for sometime] and had a love for poetry, reading and was fond of saints.

He married a girl from the Khandwalkar family, who was cultured and educated. They had three sons. Gopal Rao and his wife did their share of philanthropic deeds.

Gopal Rao helped the historian Neelkanth S. Hode Kadam and published his books on Indian history and the commentary of Shri Krishna Leela Amrit. Narayan Vaman Tilak was a poet and they welcomed him to stay in their home and gave him a portion of their Haveli so he could carry on his writing undisturbed. Shakaram B. Dhumal took Butti to Shirdi around 1908. Butti was overwhelmed by Baba's divine personality and was changed for life. He made frequent visits to Shirdi, often with his family. As there were only two wadas for staying, he decided to build a small wada for himself and his family. The rest is history. He built the wada that Baba lovingly called Dagdi Wada, which is now Samadhi Mandir. Details are given in *Shri Sai Satcharita* –Chapter 39.

Numerous leelas about Gopal Rao are given in the *Shri Sai Satcharita*. If each and everyone is mentioned it will be a small booklet. Gopal Rao though extremely wealthy and educated was meek and humble before Baba. He just humbly looked at Baba's feet and was silent.

Once an astrologer came for Baba's darshan. He handed a book on astrology to Baba, hoping He would return it with His blessings. Baba however handed the book to Butti. Although Butti did not know astrology still read it as Baba had given it to him. Soon he became proficient in astrology and many of his devotees came to him for consultations and his predictions proved true.

Unfortunately after a short illness, Butti took samadhi in 1927 at the tender age of forty-five. The illness had ravaged his body and he could not bear it any more. Just before his death he felt better for about two days. At once he called Shama, as he had intense faith in him. And as Baba had said, "Keep Madhav Rao with you. It is as good as keeping Me with you." Gopal Rao was extremely happy to see Shama and he said, "I hope Baba takes me away soon. I know you very well. If you are near by then Baba is near by." Then he placed his head on Shama's feet. Tears of joy rolled down his cheeks and happily he breathed his last. Many valuable lessons can be learnt from Butti's life. For me it is mind boggling that he did not put up a plaque or a signboard proclaiming it to be Butti Wada or Butti Haveli nor did he bother to proclaim that he donated it to the Shirdi Sai Baba Sansthan .In 1917 Butti spent lakhs of rupees to build his home or the Samadhi Mandir and quietly gave it for Baba's devotees.

The Shirdi Sai Baba Sansthan has the following written on the entrance to the Samadhi Mandir. .

Shri che Samadhi Mandir Butti Wada

Shri Sai Baba che adnana kailash vasi Shrimanth Gopal Rao Mukund rao Butti Ra Nagpur yani ha Wada swee kharchani sun 1917 Te 1918 madhye bandhlae. Vijay Dasami Shake 1840 Mangalawar ya divishi aparan vyapini Ekadishi sha 9 Dinak 15 Oct Isi sun. Tariq 9 Mohrrum Hegri sun 1825 Dhopari theen vajnacha somaras Shri Sai Baba ne Dwarkamai yethun deh tevela. Thethun tho samararambha purvak anun thyanche itche anusar yah Wadath tevana aala.

The plaque reads – According to the command of Shri Sai Baba the late Shrimanth Gopal Rao Mukund Rao Butti living in Nagpur built this wada with his own money between 1917 and 1918. On Vijayadashami, Shake 1840, that Tuesday which was Ekadasi the 15th of October [of the Hindu calendar.] and Mohrrum, the date was the 9th of Hegri Sun 1825 [of the Muslim Calendar]. In the afternoon at about 3 o'clock Shri Sai Baba left His mortal body in the Dwarkamai. From there with full ritual, and according to His wish He was placed in this wada.

Shri Sai Baba che 34th vaya punya thithi cha utsav prasanghi Is 1952 Sansthan vasasthapak Samithi tarffae Shri Santh Parnekar Maharaj yancha hasthe ya Mandir avere survarna Kalash basvayan aath aala va 36th vya punatyhya ththi utsav prasangi samaier [1954] Shrii Sai Babacha sangamraure purna kruthu Murty chi vidhi purvak sthapan sanasth vasasthapakak sanethi tharfath aale.

This plaque reads that on the thirtyfourth punyathithi utsav of Shri Sai Baba in the year 1952, the Managing Samithi Trustee, Shri Santh Parnekar Maharaj (photo 11) placed {or fix} the *suvarn* [golden] *kalash* atop this Mandir. On the thirtysixth punyatithi Utsav of 1954 the 'purna' marble idol of Shri Sai Baba was installed with full ritual and vidhi by the 'Stapan Sanstha Vasathapak Samathi.'

Leela 27:   **The Brick**

Ever since Baba came to stay in the Dwarkamai, He had a brick with Him. This brick was His constant companion. With great affection and care He looked after 'her'. Though an inanimate object, Baba loved this brick and called her His "life long companion". Baba in His characteristic way referred to it as "her". Although she was an earthen brick she was well baked and sturdy. She was one foot long, nine inches wide and three inches deep. Baba would support His hand on her while he sat in solitude in the Dwarkamai. When He slept, He used her as a pillow.

Mhalsapathy and Kashiram Shimpy would worship her by performing *mangal snan*. Then carefully place her against the pillar adjacent to the Dhuni Maa to dry. At night they would wrap her in a clean cloth and give her to Baba to use as a pillow. Though Mhalsapathy and Kashiram were constantly with Baba it did not occur to them to ask Him about the significance of this brick?

Madhu Fasle who used to sweep and clean the Dwarkamai was very careful while handling the brick. Every day he would bathe and dry her by placing her near Dhuni Maa. Later he would wrap her in a clean cloth and place her underneath the cupboard. This cupboard had Baba's clothes in it. Beneath it was a cemented platform, thus the brick would be safely stowed away. Baba loved this brick more than His life and never forgot her. Many an hour He spent with her, in self-absorption, oblivious of His surroundings.

One day when Baba had gone out a young Sevkari while sweeping the Dwarkamai accidentally dropped the brick, and she broke in two pieces. Frightened of the consequences he placed the two pieces adjacent to each other against the Dhuni Maa and left. When Baba returned He asked Mhalsapathy for His brick. Mhalsapathy lifted her and one of the broken pieces fell to the ground.

Seeing this Baba was distraught and started crying like a human being. "It's not the brick, but My fortune that is broken. She was My constant companion! Now that she has gone I too will leave." Mhalsapathy tried to comfort Him by saying, "Baba I will bind her together with a gold wire."

"O! Bhagat this brick is more valuable than many gold bricks! Now that My "Sangani" [companion] is broken I cannot remain here." Thereafter Baba's health started deteriorating and on the fifth day He took Mahasamadhi. Mention of this incident is made in *Shri Sai Satcharita* – Chapter 44. The Lord Vitthal of Pandarpur stood on a brick while the Parabhrama of Shirdi used a brick for His pillow.

I have often wondered what the significance of the brick was? Many comparisons are made to Lord Vitthal standing on a brick and Baba. The significance of the brick could possibly be, that the brick is earthern or made out of a mixture of mud and sand. Then given a shape and dried. This is symbolic of the human body. Its breaking could signify death. The brick is baked in a kiln so that it attain hardness. Nonetheless it can still break. The baking is symbolic of human nature that is enmeshed in the Ashad Vargas. Vitthal stood upon it and stamped the Ashad Vargas. While Baba kept it under His head and transferred good energy to transform Ashad Vargas from worldly emotions towards Him. An example being Kaam that emotion of love and longing can be turned towards Baba. 'This passionate love is turned towards Him, just as the Gopis loved Krishna'. As Rege says, "Its through love one should reach God especially in the beloved form of the loving Sadguru and intensely, nay passionately love Him with your heart and soul."

In 1918 when Baba took Mahasamadhi He was taken to Butti Wada according to His wish and the samadhi was made.

Madhu False, placed this broken brick as a pillow under His head. Madhu False, Shama and Tatya Kote Patil told this to Dr. Gavankar. Thus this lucky brick found her rightful place.

Leela 28:   Aare Maja Sava Rupiya!

Between Pune and Satara lies a small town called Sirval. About four hundred years ago there was a Satpurush named Narayan Swamiji. His samadhi is next to the Ram Mandir. Adjacent to his samadhi, is the samadhi of another saint Baja Bua.

Legend has it that, if a devotee worshipped the samadhi with full faith and said, "Baji dole", that Samadhi would sway. Madhav Rao Peshwa heard this and went to Shirval. And after worshipping the samadhi with full faith said, "Baji dole". And lo! the samadhi started swaying. Years later Chang Dev Maharaj went to meet Dnyaneshwar Maharaj riding on a fierce lion, using a poisonous snake for a whip. At that time Dnyaneshwar was sitting on a wall. Hearing that Chang Dev Maharaj had come to meet him he ordered the wall to move forward so he could meet him. Indeed the wall moved forth.

Years later Baba, the Parabhrama manifested in Shiladhi. He lived in a dilapidated and looked after the welfare of His devotees. One day while sitting in the masjid He said to Shama "Maje Samadhi Bole le, Maje hard Turbut thu ne Bolethil bar ka Shama" [Roughly Translated – "My Samadhi will speak, so will My bones talk to My devotees from My tomb"].

And so it came to pass that many wonderful leelas were experienced by Baba's ankita bhaktas. Some of them are given below.

Baba Sahib Tarkhad once attended the Ram Navami celebrations in the year 1932. After having a bath with utter love and devotion he went to Dwarkamai. There he took the darshan of Baba's photograph and performed puja. The puja was the offering of camphor, incense sticks and *dakshina*. After *shastang namaskar* he applied udi from Dhuni Maa. After asking Baba for permission to leave, he went to the Samadhi Mandir. There he worshipped the Samadhi and gave his dakshina. As the Ram Navami festival had concluded he decided to leave for Mumbai.

He went in time to catch the 11 a.m. bus that would have three seats vacant for pilgrims to go to Mumbai. But that day each and every bus was crowded to suffocation. So he returned to Dixit Wada. In the Wada his mind was in turmoil. Why has this happened today? Did I make any mistake in my Puja? That night his turmoil increased with every passing hour. And he was quite restless.

The next day he went to Dwarkamai to take darshan of Baba's Photograph. To his utter surprise he saw Baba's Narsingh Roop [*Angry form*] in the photograph. He was shocked and speechless. He knew in his heart that he had erred somewhere. But where? Then Baba Sahib went to Samadhi Mandir, and placed his head on Baba's padukas and no sooner had he done this he heard Baba say "Arre Maja Sava Rupiya"! At once he remembered the conversation, he had with his daughter-in-law before leaving Mumbai. She had given him one and a quarter rupees and asked him to put it in the Samadhi Mandir's dakshina box. He had tried to dissuade her, by saying, "If you put the money in the dakshina box, it will go to the Shirdi Sai Baba Sansthan general fund. But if I give it to the donation counter and get a receipt, your name will be published in their donors list in the *Sai Leela magazine*". To which she had replied, "I do not care for my name to be publicised. I am offering this money with love and devotion. All I want is that this money be put in the dakshina box" Then Baba Sahib humbly put the money in the dakshina box.

[Ref: *Shiladhi by* Dr K.B.Gavankar published by Shirdi Sai Baba Sansthan]

Balaji Pilaji Guruv had some wonderful experiences. He states that one day they were playing cards in the gallery of the Samadhi Mandir when they heard the sound of the veena. They looked around but no one was near. So they went down, the music was coming from the mosquito net over the Samadhi. They heard the most beautiful celestial symphony of the veena emitting from the samadhi. The music lasted for about ten minutes.

On another occasion, after Ram Navami, there was water oozing from the samadhi. They checked the samadhi, which was intact. The water flowed in a thin stream over the samadhi. They caught the water and used it as teerth. This lasted for about a month and then stopped.

Leela 29: Bala Krishna Keshev Vaidya alias Dada Maharaj Patgaonkar

He hailed from a small village, called Patgaon, near Rajapur (Ratnagiri District). He was a follower of the Nav Nath (Shri Jaalander Sampradaya). Spiritually advanced, he was famous in that region for his kind and loving nature.

Many a poor and downtrodden, he helped, and set them on the "Bhakti Marg". But most of all he was known for exorcising evil spirits. He and Baba were contemporaries, but had never met. Yet they knew, everything about each other, in fact they had telepathic communication with each other.

There was a householder in Mumbai who was possessed by an evil spirit. This spirit tormented the man and made him very violent. So that he caused bodily harm to his relatives. The family tried various remedies, but to no avail. As the violence increased each day they restrained him by tying him with a rope. Under such circumstances they brought him to Shirdi.

Seeing him Baba said, "Arre he is possessed by a mighty demon. I don't have a cure for him. Take him to Bala of Patgaon, and tell Dada Maharaj that I have sent him." Heeding Baba's advice the family searched for Patgaon and took him there. It took them a full fifteen days to reach there. On the day of their arrival, Dada Maharaj told all his near and dear devotees that Baba was sending a violent mad person to him. The family had never seen Dada before, and as Dada did not wear the Sanyasin's ochre robe they did not recognise him. But the householder recognised him and fell at his feet.

Dada kept the man with him for eight days, and cured him of his demonic spirits. The householder left Patgaon in a calm and serene state of mind.

On one occasion, some of his devotees went to Patgaon for his darshan, while leaving they decided to go to Shirdi. Hearing this Dada Maharaj was filled with joy. Giving them a Zari Pheta [gold embroidered cloth used as a turban] he said, "Give this cloth in Baba's hand, Do Namaskar, but do not say anything." Accordingly the devotees went to Shirdi took Baba's darshan and placed the cloth in Baba's hand. They stood aside with folded hands. On receiving the cloth Baba danced with joy saying, "My Bala has sent Me a Zari Dhoti. How nice of him." Then He tied the pheta on His head and showed it to every bhakta that came to the Dwarkamai saying, "Look! My Bala has sent this lovely Dhoti for Me".

Leela 30: **Vishnu Ghati**

Vishnu Ghati was a devotee of Dada Maharaj. He lived in a small village called Mutata, which was in Vijay Durg. Every Thursday he visited Patgaon. After taking darshan of Maharaj, he would invite him to his home. And every time Maharaj

1. Bannye Mia

2. Darga of Bannye Mia

3. Peer Maulana Sahib
(SSC, Chap 21)

4. Darga of Peer Maulana Sahib (SSC, Chap 21)

5. Mauli Sahib (SSC, Chap 14)

6. Gangagir Maharaj (SSC, Chap 5)

7. Tajuddin Baba (SSC, Chap 41)

8. Tajuddin Baba's Darga

9. Narsingh Maharaj (SSC, Chap 33)

10. Dev Baba (Leela 1)

11. Santh Parnekar (Leela 26)

12. Vakratund Maharaja

13. Krishnaji Kashinath Joshi
(Kusha Bhau) (Leela 12)

14. Kusha Bhau's Samadhi (Leela 12)

15. Uddhavesh alias
Shyamdas Baba (Leela 7)

16. Uddhavesh's Kafni (Leela 7)

17. Bappaji Lakshman Ratna
Parke (Leela 20)

18. Muley Shastri (Leela 24)

19. Gholap Swami (Leela 25)   20. Gholap Swami Mandir (Nasik) (Leela 25)

21. Vishwanath Lakshman
← Nulkar (Leela 18)

22. Portrait of Baba given
to Nana Sahib →

23. Anandrao
← Pakharde
(Leela 39)

→

24. Portrait of Baba in
Pakharde's home
(Leela 39)

25. Abdul Jan Pathan (Leela 80)

26. Damodar Vaman Atwale (Leela 35)

27. Dr. Jaganath Pandit (Leela 17)

28. Kaka Puranik (Leela 17)

29. Lakshman Kacheswar
Jakardi (Baba's pujari)

30. Yaswant Narayan Gorakshar

31. Harish Chandra R. Pithale (Leela 58)

32. Dwarkanath Pithale (Leela 59)

33. Lakshmi Bai Chinchnikar (Leela 79)

34. Savitri Bai Tendulkar
(Leela 74)

35. Raghunath Tendulkar (Leela 74)

36. Madhav Rao Tendulkar (Bapu)
(Leela 74)

37. Nana Sahib Chandorkar
(Leela 8)

38. Mahadev N. Chandorkar
(Bapu) (Leela 75)

39. Vasudev N. Chandorkar

40. Samadhi of K.J. Bhishma in
Mohappa near Nagpur (Leela 78)

41. Murlidhar Temple in Mohappa

42. Samadhi of Siddique Phalke in
Kalyan (Leela 15)

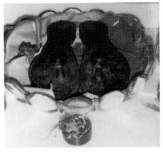

43. Khadaws (Leela 14)

44. Silver Padukas Given to Dixit (Leela 14)

45. R. B. Purandhare's Home
(Leela 77)

46. Datta Mandir (Dadar) (Leela 77)

47. Baba's Silver Idol (Leela 77)

48. Coins Given to Purandhare (Leela 77)

49. Dada Sahib Khaparde
(Leela 78)

50. Devi Das, Baal Krishna and
Balwant Kharpade (L-R)

51. Gopal Rao Somnath Nimonkar
(Leela 71)

52. Baba in procession to Lendi Baugh
(the small child is G.R Nimonkar)

53. Ramachandra M. Adkar
(Leela 70)

54. Balaram Dhurandar

Baba's Miraculous Pockets

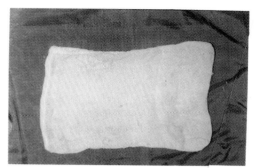

55. Jyotindra Tarkhad (Leela 14)

56. Pocket Belonging to Jyotindra (Leela 73)

57. Tatya Kote Patil

58. Pocket Belonging to Tatya (Leela 73)

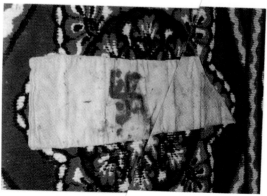

59. Pocket Belonging to the Kote Family (Leela 73)

60. Madhav Rao Deshpande
(Shama) (Leela 63)

61. Neelkant Sahasrabudhe
(Leela 16)

62. Portrait of Baba in
Shivaji Nagar Mandir
(Pune)

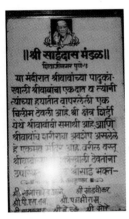

63. Plaque in Baba's
Shivaji Nagar Mandir

64. Baba's Tooth and
Chillum in Shivaji Nagar
Mandir (Leela 33)

65. Ramachandra Dada Patil
(Leela 14)

66. Sarojini Muley (Leela 72)

67. Photograph of Ram Baba
(Leela 81)

68. Chand Bhai's Samadhi
(SSC, Chap 5)

69. Chand Bhai Patil's Home
(Dhoopkhed)

70. Mahohar Mankar and his Wife

71. Anandnath Swami
(SSC, Chap 5)

72. Shyamkaran with Khagjewale (trainer)
(Leela 14)

73. Tata Building, Mumbai
(Leela 73)

74. Khalbatta for Baba's
Tambul (Leela 14)

75. Rare photograph of Baba
Going to Lendi Baugh

76. Anand Ashram (Pune)

77. Das Ganu Maharaja's
Vastra Samadhi (Gorte)

78. Baba Sahib Rudra
(Leela 82)

79. Das Ganu Maharaj (Leela 1)

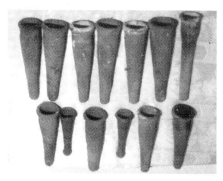

80. Baba's Magical chillums

81. Gopal Rao M Butti (Leela 26)

82. Baba's Samadhi after Niryan

83. Butti Wada or Samadhi Mandir in Recent Times (Leela 26)

84. Baba's Samadhi before 1954

85. Bird's Eye View of Samadhi Mandir

86. Baba's Portrait in Lakshmi Bai's Home

87. Baba Worshipped by B.V. Dev

88. Baba in Dabolkar's Home

89. Baba in Purandhare's
Home (Leela 77)

90. Jaikar's Painting of Baba in
Chandra Bai Borkar's Home

92. Baba hugged this photograph before giving it to Vishnu Pant Pithale →

91. Baba sent this painted portrait to Saddubhaiyya on 8th February 1915

→

93. Original photo of Baba belonging to the Mankars'

94. Original photograph of Baba belonging to Nulkar

95. Photograph used by Talim to sculpt idol in Samadhi Mandir

would say he would come, but it never came to pass. This went on for a long time. One Thursday Vishnu Ghate after darshan said, "Maharaj tell me for sure whether you will visit my home or not? Let me know one way or the other." Maharaj said, "I will surely visit your home in fifteen days. In the meantime you go to Shirdi." So Vishnu Ghate made all arrangements and went to take permission from Dada Maharaj. Dada Maharaj while sending him off gave him two packets of peda. Maharaj said, "Give the larger packet of pedas to Baba, and the smaller packet you share with your family. Also do not keep all your money in one pocket. For if it's stolen you will lose all your money." Vishnu said "All right" and left.

He went home to pack his bags. In the excitement he packed the smaller packet of pedas in the baggage. Then he distributed the larger packet to all the members of his family. As it would have taken him many days to reach Shirdi, Dada advised him to place his money in various pockets. But when he reached Mumbai, he forgot what Maharaj had advised and placed all his money in one pocket.

On reaching Shirdi he went to the Dwarkamai for Baba's darshan. There was a large gathering of devotees around Baba. Nonetheless he managed to go to the Sanctum Sanctorum. After doing namaskar to Baba he handed the packet of pedas to Him. Baba took the packet and looked at it from every side, and then in anger shouted, "Arre You ate up My packet of pedas which was larger of the two. Now you are trying to palm off this packet on Me?"

A volley of abuses followed this, then Baba said, "Rascal do I owe anything to your father? Why do you keep calling Me to your home? Do you think I have nothing else to do? Remember this if you ever call Me again to your house then you will have to bear the consequences! If you want, you come here! You need to be taught a lesson." Then Baba took the money that he had in his pocket, which in fact was all the money he had. Then Baba said, "You don't know how great

My Bala is! He is Shankar. He is Dutta. He is your only refuge. Now go tomorrow."

Vishnu trembled with fear. He wondered how Baba knew that he had asked Dada Maharaj to visit his home! In a flash he realised that that though Dada lived far away, yet Baba and he were in communication. And he, Vishnu was just a puppet whose strings were in Dada's hands. He also got an insight of Baba's omnipresence.

He fell at Baba's feet and begged forgiveness saying, "Baba I am your child have mercy on me. You are my mother, so give me refuge at Your feet." Hearing his piteous cry Baba's heart melted and He stroked his back and hugged him and asked him to sit in the Sabha Mandap. Vishnu got up and sat against the wall of the Sabha Mandap. His stomach started rumbling with hunger, and he had no money. While leaving Mumbai he had put all his money in one pocket; forgetting the advice given by Dada. He was in a fix, he knew no one here and he had no money even to buy a return ticket. Just then a well-dressed gentleman came and sat next to him and casually conversed with him. Vishnu was surprised when he said that he was going to Mumbai so Vishnu should accompany him. Then he said, " Now lets go and have lunch. Then we will rest and leave for Mumbai in the morning." He took care of Vishnu's every need and was a gracious host. The next morning they left for Mumbai. At Mumbai, Vishnu was surprised that his gracious host was lost in the crowd. Vishnu stayed in Mumbai for two days then returned home.

The day after he reached home, he went to Patgaon. He took darshan of Dada Maharaj and fell at his feet and said "Maharaj if you wanted to teach me a lesson, why couldn't you have taught it to me here." Dada Maharaj replied, "Only a goldsmith should pierce the ear." Thus Vishnu realised how much regard Maharaj had for Baba. He remained devoted to both of them.

In 1941, on the sixth of Kartik month Dada Maharaj took Samadhi.

Leela 31:   **Pangya and the Coin**

Santhathanay lived in Mumbai with his family. His younger brother was four-years-old when he started getting convulsions. The family tried all kinds of medicines and pills but of no avail. Once a friend of the family suggested electrotherapy. They took the child to the doctor who inserted a small rod below his ear. The doctor promised them that the child would be convulsion free in a few days. But no such thing happened. To add to the child's misery, he started running a high temperature. Again a slew of doctors came and gave medical aid. But the fever continued. After a few days the child took a turn for the worse. He became cold and clammy, his pulse was feeble and he was in a state of shock. Again the doctors were summoned. After giving some treatment they gave up hope. A friend of the family happened to stop by. Seeing the distraught state of the family he suggested that they pray to Baba. The brother at once went and stood in front of Baba's photograph, and earnestly sent a prayer. About an hour later, the boy stared sweating profusely. He cried out loudly saying, "Baba has come and He is calling me. Pangya do not worry you will be all right." Then Santhathanay remembered he had taken his brother a year ago to Shirdi and Baba had called him "Pangya" and given him a coin. Following this incident the child recovered from the high fever and gradually the convulsive disorder also abated.

Leela 32:   **Baba Gave His Tooth to Kashi Bai**

The bridegroom was from Niphad so Kashi Bai left her parents home in Shirdi and accompanied her husband at Niphad. She was quite happy at her in-laws home. They were farmers and were economically stable. A year later, her husband died. At that time Kashi Bai was pregnant. A son was born and she named him Madhav. When Madhav was five months old she returned to Shirdi and stayed with her parents. Kashibai did all the household chores and looked after Madhav.

Her parents were rather poor, when Madhav was about two-years-old, she decided to work in the fields. Every day she brought Madhav to Dwarkamai early in the morning and then went to work. At dusk she used to take Madhav home. Thus Madhav was left entirely in Baba's care. When Madhav became four-years-old he started doing chores for Baba. Baba gave him one rupee daily. Kashi Bai however struggled trying to make both ends meet. One day when she came to pick up Madhav, she accosted Baba and said, "Baba, you give all and sundry huge amounts of money. How come you give my Madhav but one rupee? Even though he does your chores, this is not fair." Baba replied calmly, "The money I give to others can stop at any time, but I will never stop giving money to Madhav. "Me Tumche Sarkya anathi mahile cha matti aahe" [I am the saviour of destitute women like you].

Kashi Bai could not understand what Baba was saying and she yelled, "Oh my husband and matti died five years ago". Baba flew into a rage hearing this. Seeing his ferocious form Kashi Bai stealthily took Madhav home. Frightened, she did not go to masjid for two to three days. Baba however kept

88

asking where Madhav was? Then he sent a messenger to fetch him. Kashi Bai and Madhav came to Dwarkamai and stood meekly before Baba. Baba smiled and beckoned to them to come close.

Then gently pulling out one of his loose tooth, he placed it in a handful of udi. Then he tied it in an old rag and gave it to Kashi Bai saying, 'Keep this safely with you, Allah bhala karega. (Allah will do good).' On returning home, Kashi Bai made a talisman of the tooth and udi and tied it around Madhav's right arm. When Kashi Bai died Madhav Rao decided to go with his family to Niphad.

Leela 33: How did Baba's Tooth Became Enshrined in Shivaji Nagar Temple in Pune

Damodar Rasne (Dammu Anna – *Shri Sai Satcharita*, Chapter 25) who lived in Ahmed Nagar moved with his family to Pune. They bought a *chawl* (multi-storeyed building) in Shivaji Nagar. His son, Nana Sahib bought two rooms in that chawl and converted it into shrine in 1945. Devotees from far and near flocked there to attend aarti and festivals. Gradually their numbers increased. On Thursdays and festivals the shrine was packed to suffocation. Nana Sahib realised that soon a temple would have to be build to accommodate the devotees. He sought the help of another devotee named Nicam. Nicam was working in the Police Department in Khed and upon Nana Sahib's request he resigned and came to Pune.

A small temple was built in front of Rasne chawl and Baba's photograph was worshipped with due formalities. Nicam put his energy into the building of the temple. He also looked after the care and maintenance of it and the overall administration. One night he had a vivid dream in which Baba told him to go to Niphad and get His tooth from Madhav.

This was easy, as he had met Madhav Rao several times at Shirdi. Simultaneously Madhav Rao dreamt of Baba who said, "Give the tooth to the person who will come to you tomorrow." Nicam went to Madhav Rao's home in Niphad and found Madhav Rao waiting for him. Madhav Rao was surprised to hear about Nicam's dream and he happily handed over the talisman.

In 1950, Shri B.V. Narasimha Swamiji did the *sthapana* of the photograph and Baba's tooth and chillum (photo 64). The tooth and chillum are housed in the 'Silver Paduka' of Baba in the temple.

Leela 34: **Lakshmi Bai Ganesh Khaparde**

Lakshmi Bai was a gentle, cultured, kind, affluent and devout lady. Gajanan Maharaj was her Guru. Before he took samadhi he directed his devotees to go to Shirdi assuring them that Baba would look after their "Samsarik and Adhyatmak" welfare splendidly. Many a devotee like Khaparde, Dhumal and Butti came to Shirdi on the Maharaj's advice.

The *rinanubandh* between Lakshmi Bai and Baba was unfathomable. In 1912, Lakshmi Bai came to Shirdi and stayed for seven months while her husband stayed for four months. Daily she prepared '*Bogh*' for Baba and only after Baba accepted naivedya and partook of it, did she have her meal.

On 4th March, 1912 she was rather late in bringing the naivedya. Baba perceiving her utter love and devotion bend the rule a bit. The rule being of prohibiting females from entering the Sanctum Sanctorum after the curtains were drawn.

He not only allowed Lakshmi Bai to come up with the platter but also to do *charanseva*. The incident is beautifully described in the *Shri Sai Satcharita,* Chapter 27. Baba eats the food eagerly being indifferent to many a platter full of delicious savouries and "Panch Pakewan". Shyama becomes curious about this and asked Baba, "Why this partiality?"

Baba said, "Shyama how can I describe the excellence of this food." Baba then describes four of her previous births. Each birth had a strong bond of love and devotion towards Him. Baba voraciously eats the food and belches expressing His satiety. Lakshmi Bai then does 'Charan Seva.' Baba in turn gently presses the hands that were massaging His feet. This was transference of the *Shakti Pathi.* He told her softly to say "Rajaram Rajaram." And this she said till the end of her life.

Leela 35: Damodar Vaman Atwale alias Dammu Anna

The rinanubandh for Das Ganu was intense and passionate. But Baba's grace extends to Das Ganu's adopted son and disciple. The touching story is narrated below.

Whenever Das Ganu went to Pune and stayed with Vaman Rao Podar in Jageshwari lane. Once Das ganu was standing near a window in Poddar's house. He looked at the street below and saw a young lad of about nine-years crying bitterly. The reason being that the boy had just completed his *madhukari* or *bhiksha* rounds and was returning home. On his way he was touched by a lowly *tonga wala* (driver). He was thus polluted, and hence could not partake of the food. In those days untouchability was rampant along with orthodoxy and superstition. The boy was at his wits end as the thought of going hungry loomed before him. Das Ganu was astonished to see that in a city like Pune, the boy managed to lead an orthodox life. Das Ganu being a kind symphathetic man asked the boy to dine with him. He assured Dammu anna that when he was at Poona he need not worry about his meals. On hearing this the boy's face lit up and he prostrated at Das Ganu's feet.

Das Ganu felt a deep bond with the boy whose handsome face glowed and his bright lustrous eyes spoke of his gratitude. Das Ganu laid his hand on the boy's head and caressed his back. The boy's eyes filled with tears at the tenderness showed by Das Ganu. Das Ganu gently asked him about his life. Damodar told him that he hailed from a village called Guhagar in Konkan. He had come to Pune to study the Vedas. And was staying with his brother. Although his brother owned a sawmill, he was not interested in his welfare. Hence he went for biksha. Damodar (photo 26) had two great qualities, his handwriting was perfect and his voice was very melodious. Das Ganu expressed his voice thus 'his voice was like a tinkling bell and the high notes could reach the heights of a mountain.' Both these qualities endeared him to Das Ganu who had the habit of asking others to write, while he spoke the text. The year was 1905 and Das Ganu was on his last chapter of *Arvachin Bhakti Leelamruth*. So Damodar could write for him. Secondly, Dammu Anna would join him in his keertan. Thus Dammu Anna became his disciple, and a perfect disciple he was. The *rinanubandh* between them was great. As Das Ganu had no children of his own he adopted Dammu Anna. Together they went for keertans. Damu Anna would stand behind Das Ganu and intently listen to what he sang. Once he heard the keertan, he could sing the same from his memory. He also inculcated the morale of the keertan and lived life along those lines. In short, he was a perfect disciple and son. Often when he sang, he was in absolute bliss, and crowds flocked to hear their keertans. When they came to Das Ganu after the keertan to felicitate him, he would pass the credit to his son.

Das Ganu was a prolific writer, and he had decided to write the *Santh Charita*, i.e. Life of Saints. Thus he had to travel from place to place to gather material. So, he decided to leave his son with Nana Sahib Chandorkar who was residing at Ahmed Nagar. Nana being magnanimous took Dammu Anna and looked after him like his own son, and nothing was wanting.

Once Nana took Dammu to Shirdi. On seeing him Baba said, "Arre Nana why are you keeping Ganu's son with you. The father should look after his son. Why are you getting involved in his *samsarik* life? Let him go to his father." Nana an ardent devotee of Baba considered His words as law and sent Dammu Anna back to Das Ganu after one and half years of caring for him. When Das Ganu went to Shirdi he asked Baba why He had done so. Baba said, "Arre, Why is your son with Nana, you take care of your son, God is concerned and will take care of you." Thus Baba sowed the seed for the book *Shisyabodh*, which various Gurus use as a text and reference book even today. At that time Das Ganu was forty-three and Dammu was a young man. When Das Ganu wrote his *shisyabodh*, Dammu Anna memorised and followed the teaching thereof to the letter. Simultaneously Dammu's voice became ever so melodious and their fame reached far and wide. Thus Das Ganu gave Dammu Anna *Shishyabodh*. He gave Dammu Anna's son *Chatrabodh* (teaching for students). Das Ganu being a loving father and a perfect guru wanted Dammu Anna to get settled in life. Once Das Ganu and Dammu Anna went to Shirdi and there Dammu Anna sang a bhajan – "Ghar Jane deo, Jane Shyam murari," (Let me go home, do let me go home, Sham Murari). He sang the bhajan with such love and devotion that Baba's eyes brimmed with tears. Nana Sahib Chandorkar, Kaka Dixit, Kaka Mahajani and many other bhaktas were present. And all of them were moved to tears by his rendition.

In fact, Kaka Dixit wrote in his diary that Baba liked the bhajan so much that he was fully immersed in it. He asked

Dammu Anna to sing it four times. There was a huge crowd of devotees for the bhajan. Amongst the crowd were Dr. Mahabal, his wife, and daughter. After the bhajan Baba pointing to the doctor said to Das Ganu, "Ganu why don't you get Dammu married to the Daughter of Dr. Mahabal?" The doctor was astonished to hear Baba's words and he kept quiet.

After the darshan, the doctor and his family left for Sangolia. There he was quite restless as Baba's words kept echoing in his ears. In 1914, Dammu Anna was married to Dr.Mahabal's daughter Kamala. With Baba's blessing the marriage went of well. Baba Himself came for the marriage and threw *akshatha* on the bride and groom. Kamala was renamed Radha. Radha and Dammu lead a peaceful and happy married life. As time passed by a son named Anantha Rao was born to them.

Then a tragedy struck them. Dammu Anna became ill with tuberculosis. Das Ganu spent a lot of money and got the best doctors from Bombay and Pune to treat him. Das Ganu tried everything under the sun to bring relief to his favourite shishya (student). But the disease was relentless. Finally he took Damu Anna and his family to Pandarpur. He made a small hut in the compound of his home for the family to stay in. Further, in case Dammu Anna needed help at night, he tied a bell in the room which was accessible to Dammu Anna who had just to ring it and Das Ganu would be there to help.

Then on *paush, shuklapaksh, Dashami* 1924, early in the morning the bell started ringing loudly and Dammu Anna was calling to Das Ganu. Immediately Das Ganu went to the hut, and a whole lot of people also gathered there. Dammu Anna was sitting on the bed listless and drained. As soon as Das Ganu entered the room, Dammu Anna got down and prostrated at Das Ganu's feet. He never got up as he had breathed his last at the feet of his Guru.

The kindness of Das Ganu had no boundaries. He looked after Radha and Anantha Rao as a father would. Anantha Rao was indeed fortunate to sit on Das Ganu's lap and play with him he as he grew up. Das Ganu asked him to take sanyas but he did not till Das Ganu and his mother were alive.

Leela 36:   **Mari Aai and Death**

Jyotindra Tarkhad and Baba had a very special relationship. Jyotindra loved Baba immensely and Baba reciprocated with parental love and care. The *rinanubandhic* ties between them were very deep. Jyotindra was a young lad of fourteen years and used to study in St. Xaviers School, Mumbai.

On one of his visits to Shirdi, there was an epidemic of cholera. But Jyotindra was fearless, as he had intense faith in Baba. He was certain that nothing would happen to him, as Baba was there to protect him. He went about doing his rituals as usual. Jyotindra used to light petromax lamps and place them in the Dwarkamai daily. One evening after having completed this chore he was entering the Sanctum Sanctorum when Baba flew into a rage. He started shouting at him angrily. Baba said that He would cut him into seven pieces and bury him in the Dwarkamai. Jyotindra was scared and begged Baba for forgiveness lest he had done something wrong. This further infuriated Baba, or so it seemed, and His anger reached its zenith. Then Baba ordered Jyotindra to press His legs.

Immediately, he started pressing his legs with great devotion. Suddenly, he saw a fiendish looking woman in front of him. She was so terrifying to look at that he had no words of description. Instinctively he clutched Baba's feet tightly. Baba on the other hand was saying something to her. The verbal volley continued for sometime, but he could not comprehend what was being said. He was so frightened that he lost consciousness. After a while she disappeared.

Jyotindra finally regained consciousness, and realised that Baba was shaking him and asking him to get up. Baba said, "Arre Bhau I asked you to press My legs, but you are holding them so tightly that your nails are piercing Me". Then Jyotindra asked for some water, and Baba gave him some from the *matka* (earthen pot). Baba also told him that for the next four days he may not be able to ingest any food and he should rethink whether he should continue coming to Shirdi or not? Baba said, "Tell Me exactly what you saw just now." Jyotindra could not formulate the word at that moment. Gently, Baba asked, "Arre Bhau tell Me what you saw?" Jyotindra said, "Baba, don't show me such terrifying things." Then Baba said, "She was 'Mari Aai', the goddess of ill omen, and misfortune. She had set her heart on taking you away." Then reassuringly, He added, "But I would not allow her, and I let her take five others instead". Hearing this he was overwhelmed, and he laid his head on Baba's feet.

Jyotindra was rarely sick, but in the month of July 1965 he fell ill. He had bronchitis, and developed severe muscle spasm, of the waist. This forced him to lie in bed. The pain was so severe that even after the application of analgesic creams it would not abate. Jyotindra was saddened by the thought that his son had to apply the cream and nurse him. Gradually his condition worsened, and he lost his muscle tone and was admitted at the Nanavati hospital for about a week. On the last *Shravan Somwar* (*Shravan* is August by the Hindu calendar and *Somwar* is Monday which is considered extremely holy), he asked for tea and drank it. After a short while later, he asked for tea again. His wife gently reminded him that she had just given him his tea.

"Yes! But I want some tea as I am seeing someone, and I can't discern who it is?" he replied. Tea was sent for and while waiting his wife said, "While the tea comes, why don't you do Baba's *naamsmaran?*" Then Jyotindra said, "Someone is calling me, but I cannot see the face clearly." His wife gave him the *tulsi maala* for doing *jaap*, (to continuously take The Lords name), and she applied *udi* on his forehead.

He started *naamsmaran*, and after a short while, he saw Baba. So, he folded his hands and did *namaskar*. "Baba, Mee

Aalo (Baba, I'm coming)," he said. Then he closed his eyes and took *samadhi* (died) peacefully with Baba in front of him.

No more needs to be said about this *rinanubandh* relationship.

Leela 37: The Leela of the Evil Spirit

"Get up from here," said a voice in a loud confrontational manner. The devotee looked around but could not see anyone at first. Rather confused, he wondered where the person was who gave him this order. It was *purnima* (full moon night) and he could see everything clearly. The ground itself was bathed in the moonlight and even a pinhead could be found in the brightness. It was a little past midnight and the devotee had gone outside to relieve himself. He was behind the banyan tree behind Dixit wada. A little later, he heard something rustling amongst the fallen leaves. Thinking it might be a snake he became alert. Then he noticed 'the spirit' who was clothed in a white garment and looked like a man. The spirit spoke again, "This is my territory, so you better leave." The devotee looked with great concentration, as he was afraid. But the spirit added, "You are rather confident of the old man's grace (Baba's grace) and protection, aren't you?" As soon as this was said, the devotee stood up, and was calm. "Yes, come closer and show yourself." The spirit started moving closer and was about two to three feet away from the devotee.

"Stop right there or I'll call Baba and He will reduce you to ashes", warned the devotee. Hearing this, the spirit rose to the top of the tree and disappeared. The devotee walked back to his room. At first, he thought that he would tell his mother about the incident, but fearing that she might be frightened, he kept quiet. The next morning, after bathing, he went to Dwarkamai, and prostrated before Baba and sat down quietly.

"Bhau, what did you see last night," asked Baba. "Baba, I saw a ghost," said the devotee. Then Baba said, "Arre Bhau that was Me". The puzzled devotee replied, "No Baba, it was a ghost, and I spoke to it." "It was Me Bhau, ask your mother," said Baba. The devotee turned to his mother, who said, "Yes, Baba is in everything – man, bird, beast, and spirits too." Besides, spirits are in Baba's control. Thus, the devotee, Baba Sahib Tarkhad learnt a very valuable lesson.

[Ref: *Sai Leela,* Ank 1-2, Year 8, 1930]

Leela 38: **Vinayak Shankar Giridhar**

He was a 'Talathi' (A Talathi is a government official who keeps records of land deeds, ration cards and domicility of the residents by profession) and in 1912 he was transferred to Gondvile near Andheri [Mumbai]. There he lived in a *chawl* near Mukund Sadashiv Patil's temple with his family. After coming to Andheri he met Ramachandra Sitaram Dev and they became good friends. Dev told him about Baba, and asked him to have His darshan. His first visit to Shirdi was in summer of that year, and he stayed for three days. About three months later, the monsoons started and it rained in torrents, and there was water everywhere. Giridhar lived in front of the building, next-door was a grocery store and behind this a room was being built. The foundation was to be completed, so they had excavated an area that was about six feet deep and two feet wide. Work was stopped because of the rains. The incessant rain had filled that area and the water in the pit was rising.

One evening his three-year-old son was playing in the rain. After some time he put on his cap, took an umbrella and went to the rear of the house. Accidentally he fell into the pit of the foundation. His mother was unaware of this. A little while later she started looking for him and couldn't find him.

So she went to the back of the building, only to find him climbing out of the pit. There was no body around, the boy was thoroughly soaked, but not hurt. Terrified at what might have happened, she brought him into the house and changed his clothes. By then a crowd had gathered there. Giridhar returned home from work just then and saw the commotion. Later he asked his son how he managed to climb out of there. His son told him that they had made steps for this. A day prior to this incident Giridhar had a dream, wherein his son was laying still and he and his wife were crying. Then Baba appeared and said, " The boy is sleeping, and so what is this sorrow all about"? As his son had not drowned, nor was hurt in any way, Giridhar's faith in Baba increased by leaps and bounds.

Once he, Ramachandra Sitaram Dev and Ganesh Pandurang Bendre went on a pilgrimage to Shirdi. Before leaving his wife Giridhar gave her a rose garland to offer to Baba. This garland she strung together with great love and devotion. On reaching Shirdi, they went to the Dwarkamai. Giridhar after prostrating before Baba garlanded Him. Baba said, "This garland is made with love and devotion." Much to Giridhar's surprise Baba kept the garland for a long time, while He quickly disposed off other garlands that were offered. That night Baba appeared in his wife's dream and said, "This garland that you have made for Me is full of love. Keep offering Me such garlands time and again."

On another occasion he along with his son, Dev and Bendre went to Shirdi. They had the Darshan of Baba. Giridhar then made his son do *sashtang namaskar*. While the child was doing so Giridhar mentally prayed to Baba saying, "Baba this child is Yours please take care of him." Eight years later in

1922 the boy came down with Plague. A short while before this Giridhar was transferred to Bandra, while his wife and son were at Agaasi.

He got the news about the illness from his brother-in -law, who had just returned from Agaasi. Hearing this he immediately went to Agaasi. There he found his son in a precarious condition. The child [name not given] was running a very high temperature, was delirious, and could hardly breathe. Dr Dinkar Jaganath Galvankar was treating him. Daily he would make home-visits. He gave him an injection twice a day. Giridhar prayed to Baba with his heart and soul. He placed a photograph of Baba near his pillow, and earnestly said, "Baba cure this child quickly and we will come and take darshan of Your Samadhi." He also applied Baba's *udi* morning and night to the child. But nothing seemed to go right. For the first three days it seemed that the doctor could not control the case. Giridhar was in a terrible state of mind and did not know what to do. But Baba's grace was with his son. On the eleventh day when the doctor came and gave the injection he said, "Don't worry he will recover." However the treatment continued for several days. At last the fever abated, following this, the bubos burst and his son recovered.

About a year before his son got plague, his wife was seriously ill with a fulminant pneumonia. This soon turned into an epidemic, and many of his family members lost their lives. His mother-in-law was the first to pass away, followed by two nieces. Four days later, his wife's cousin contracted the disease, and passed away on the fifth day. Giridhar felt that as he had sought refuge in Baba nothing bad would happen to his wife. Dr Dinkar Jaganath Galvankar treated his wife, and he would visit the home twice a day. Then one day his elder sister-in-law got a dream in which Baba in the form of Dattatreya came and filled her ' Ootie' [To put auspicious gift in the *pallou* of the Saree] with Haldi [tumeric]. This was a sign that all would go well, Indeed that very day Giridhar started recovering. Steadily his fever and cough got better.

Before Baba took Mahasamadhi, Giridhar's wife got a dream in which Baba appeared and said, "Take your child outside and give him a bath." But they could not understand the meaning of this. At that time they were staying in a village called Manori. After sometime they went to Bandra. There Giridhar heard that on *vijay dashami* Baba took samadhi. Then he realised the meaning of the dream. [In Maharashtra when a person passes away, their near and dear ones bathe outside their home].   [Ref: *Sai Leela*, Ank 11, Year 3, 1925]

Leela 39:   **Anandrao Pakharde**

A nandrao Pakharde (photo 23) was a famous businessman in 1910. In those days, very few Maharashtrians used to do business. He lived on Lamington Road. Being an astute businessman, he bought a bungalow in Vile Parle, Nehru Road in 1914. Vile Parle was then a desolate place with only four houses. There was no electricity or water supply. The family used a lantern and drank well water. This state of affairs induced him to form the property owners' association. He was the president of the Association for many years. He diligently worked to make the suburb of Vile Parle into a modern beautiful place. A crossroad near his home has honoured him by naming it Pakharde Chowk. Dixit lived next door and they were friends. Dixit being a devotee of Sai Baba often spoke of His leelas. It was Dixit who was instrumental in Anandrao's going to Shirdi. In *Shri Sai Satcharita,* Chapter 45 the beautiful leela of his dream vision of Baba is given.

Once Pakharde had a dream vision in which he saw Baba seated on a splendid bejewelled throne. In front of Him stood Pakharde and Shama. Shama said, "Anandrao, bow at His feet." Anandrao said that was his intense desire, but Baba's feet were underwater. "O Deva, do take out your feet from the water", said Shama. Baba did so and Pakharde at once clasped His feet. Baba blessed Pakharde and added, "Give a dhotar with a silk border to My Shama, and you will enjoy peace and happiness." So, Pakharde bought a *dhotar* and gave it to Dixit to hand it over to Shama.

Anandrao had a painting of Baba (photo 24) that he prayed to. It is a family heirloom, as it was with him since Baba's sojourn in Shirdi. One does not know whether Baba himself gave it to him.

Leela 40: **Govind Damodar Pandit**

He lived in a small village called Phalse in Taluka Panvel [jilha Kulva]. Govind was distraught and anxious as he could not find a suitable match for his daughter. For two years he went hither and thither, trying to find a bridegroom. Often he took leave for three months and met friends and relatives expressing his anxiety. But no proposal came.

One day he went to his friend's home, and sat and chatted with him. The conversation turned to the great saints of Maharashtra. His friend started talking about Baba. When suddenly he said, "Govind Rao! If your daughter gets married within fifteen days, we will go to Shirdi, and have Baba's darshan." Govind Rao agreed to this and said, "All right."

Imagine his surprise, when the Harderkar family from south Hyderabad visited his home. They came looking for a prospective bride for their son. The boy met his daughter and agreed to marry her. The earliest *mahurat* (auspicious time) for marriage was fixed and the marriage took place. All this happened with him not having to go here and there. His friend reminded him, that as the marriage took place with in fifteen days, they should go for Baba's darshan.

Before leaving for Shirdi, he borrowed thirty rupees from his friend. On reaching Shirdi, they went to the Maruti Mandir, and thence to the Dwarkamai. Baba and His bhaktas had gone to Lendi Baugh. They went to the Sanctum Sanctorum, and did namaskar to the Nimbar and sat down. The devotees gathered there told them that Baba was extremely angry when He left for Lendi Baugh, so it would be wise of them to go to the Sabha Mandap, or risk being beaten by Baba. Following their advice Govind went to the Sabha Mandap, and awaited Baba's return. After a little while Baba in procession entered the Dwarkamai. Everyone in the procession was laughing and swaying, and not a trace of anger was seen on Baba's face. The devotees gathered there were surprised to see this joyous procession.

Before entering the Sanctum Sanctorum Baba said, "Bring water for My bath." At that time He was standing on the steps of the Dwarkamai. His devotees brought water and washed His feet. Govind Rao seized the opportunity and drank the paad teerth (holy water after washing the feet). Later he went up and offered a coconut, pan-supari [beetlenut and leaf], along with dakshina of one rupee. Then he placed his head on Baba's feet and did *sashtang namaskar*. "You do not have to place your head on My feet. Even if you do Namaskar from a far it will reach Me," said Baba. Hearing this Govind Rao again did Namaskar. Baba again repeated the same sentences.

Seeing the dakshina of one rupee Baba said, "Give Me another rupee. Why do you give just one rupee?" Govind Rao then gave another rupee. While doing so he handed a rupee to his friend to give to Baba. "Don't give him a rupee, he has a rupee in his pocket", said Baba, which was true.

Baba then picked up the one rupee that Govind Rao had placed before Him as dakshina. He tossed it about and looking at Govind Rao said, "I owe you thirty rupees." This He repeated several times. In actuality Baba did not owe Govind Rao any money. However Govind Rao had borrowed thirty rupees from his friend for the pilgrimage.

Bapu Sahib Jog's sister came to take Baba's darshan. Baba inquired about her welfare. Then Baba asked her where Bapu Sahib was? She replied that he was sleeping at that time. Baba then turned to one of His devotee and said, "Narayan if that Bapu Sahib comes here, give him a good thrashing. He took three to four thousand rupees from Me. And has not returned it. He keeps saying that he will return it, but never does that." Hearing this Govind was amazed, for he had loaned the same amount to a person named Bapu Sahib, who kept promising to return it, but had not.

As the time for their departure approached Baba looked at Govind Rao and said, "I will come with you. The people here trouble Me a lot". Govind Rao could not understand what Baba meant. Shama said, "What Baba said about His coming with you is true Govind Rao. Baba's presence is felt there. So He is there." Before his pilgrimage to Shirdi, Shama had visited Phalse. At that time Govind Rao had taken him around. Near his house there was a huge banyan tree, beneath which was a small Pir. Later Baba gave Govind Rao *udi*, and applied some on his forehead, and gave him permission to leave. [Ref: *Sai Leela*, Ank 4, Year 3, 1925]

Leela 41:   **Lakshmi Bai Tuse**

Shri Ram was her ishtadev and she had not even heard of Baba. That was in 1912 that she had gone to her father's house. There she performed puja to Shri Ram and Hanuman. The *devera* (miniature temple for God's idol) was placed on a shelf above. As was her daily routine she did an elaborate puja. Then she went upstairs to rest. In front of the building was a *jamun* tree. Atop that tree was a monkey, who looked bright and powerful like Hanuman. Jumping off the tree, he came to the window and then suddenly disappeared.

That night she dreamt of Baba who said, "Come to Shirdi your Ram is here. So come as often as you want." She had never heard of Shirdi. Her Guru however told her everything about Shirdi. It was in 1913 that she got a chance to visit Shirdi When she saw Baba, He was the Saint she had dreamt of.

In 1917, she visited Shirdi again. After the noon *aarti,* and meal was over, she stayed on in the Dwarkamai. Lakshmi Bai was very concerned about her property. She confided in Shama, and told him the story. She was gifted vast farmland by her father-in-law, so she could live of it comfortably. But her father had impounded the land and would not hand it over to her. Nor would he stay on the farm. Then she asked Shama if he would speak to Baba on her behalf. Shama however told her to speak for herself.

At that time Baba was standing against the wall of the Dwarkamai. He was abusing very violently. After a few minutes He went and sat in the Dwarkamai near the Katrada. Anna Chinikar was massaging His feet and Jog was doing seva. Lakshmi Bai went up and sat down, but said nothing. Baba said to Jog, "Anna has swindled Kaki and completely wiped her of all her possessions. He gives Me a lot of trouble." To which Anna replied, "I have never swindled anyone of their possessions. Nor have I ever troubled Baba". Then to Lakshmi Bai He said, " Kaki let him eat, after all it's Anna who is eating it. Do not register a complaint against him. Allah will give you enough, and there will be no dearth. You, Me and Anna will go and live in Nashik."

Lakshmi Bai was surprised to hear this. Her father's name was Anna. He had swindled her of her farmland. Many of her well-wishers had suggested that she lodge a complaint. However she followed Baba's advice. At first she had a lot of trouble, but that to passed. She completed a course in nursing and midwifery and lived comfortably.

[Ref: *Sai Leela,* Ank 4, Year 3, 1925]

Leela 42: **Shakaram Krishna Pangarkar**

His goal was to publish a magazine called *Swadurma Deep*. So he mentally set a deadline. But as circumstance would have it, he found himself in great financial difficulty. He was depressed and anxious, for he knew not where the money would come from. That night he had a vivid dream. The owner of Arya Vijay printing press came to him and said, How did you get yourself in this financial predicament? Why are you in financial difficulty? Now listen to me, near Barsi is a place called Vairung, go there. There you will find a satpurush, who will relieve you of your financial problems." As the dream continued Shakaram went there. Under a tree, he found the Satpurush. He was lying in a relaxed fashion with his palms below his head, with his feet drawn up. Shakaram prostrated, and placed his head on his feet. He prayed for respite of his problems.

The Satpurush replied in the affirmative and added "Will you bathe me". Shakaram agreed and they went to a canal nearby. Shakaram bathed him with reverence. After the bath was over, a little boy and girl appeared. They invited the Satpurush for a prasad meal. They turned to Shakaram and asked him whether he would join them. Shakaram was glad to do so. Then the group proceeded, the children lead the way followed by the Satpurush, and Shakaram in the rear. It was then that Shakaram noticed a luminous figure in front of all of them. It was the monsoon season and the vegetation was lush and green, the sky was clear and blue. They reached some farmland and continued to walk along the fringe, when he woke up suddenly. This was in the year 1910. Following this dream his financial difficulties were mysteriously resolved.

Some time later he met an old friend of his, Deo Mamlatdar of Dhanu. Shakaram had met his younger brother Ganpatrao Deo in Mumbai. Ganpatrao was studying for a medical degree at that time. Often they would have long conversations. Ganpatrao spoke about Shirdi, and Baba's leelas and divinity. He said, "If you want to know more, about Baba You should ask my elder brother. He is in Shirdi right now, you should go there and meet him." Shakaram had to go to Baroda that day so he did not make the Shirdi trip. However he did meet Baba BV Deo and related his dream to him. He responded saying that he would meet a satpurush in the future.

In 1912, Shakaram was suffering from some liver disorder. So he had gone to Dhanu to stay with a friend {Unfortunately the friends name is not mentioned}. This friend took utmost care of him and got a doctor to examine him. Shakaram took the medicines as prescribed. But his condition did not improve much. About ten days after the treatment was started his friend took him to Shirdi. When Shakaram was packing his bag, he hid the medicines amongst his belongings. Then they set out. While travelling Shakaram secretly ingested the medicines. But what awaited him was beyond his wildest imagination. They reached Kopergaon at dawn. It was *Margashish* (November), his friend went to the Godavari and had a bath. Then he made Shakaram bathe in the holy river. The water was very cold, but nothing untoward happened to him. Out of fear, and due to his weakened condition Shakaram had not bathed for the past month. They proceeded to Shirdi by *tonga*, and alighted at Dixit wada. After keeping their belongings in the wada, they went for darshan. As they climbed the steps of the Dwarkamai Baba said, "So Sowkar, you have come. How many people have you brought with you? Ten or twelve?" At that time his friend had left his family at Dixit wada and had gone for darshan alone. Indeed the family consisted of twelve members. They prostrated, and placed their head on Baba's feet and gave Baba dakshina.

His friend had a desire to give two rupees as dakshina. He thought that he would change the two rupees into four or eight anna coins. And give one each to his children to offer to Baba. But he could not get change, nor were his children with him at that time. Baba read his thought and said, "Why don't you give the two rupees dakshina right now." Shakaram thus experienced Baba's *antarjnana* (omniscient). They did Baba's *charanseva*, and got udi *prasad*. Baba gave them leave to go to the wada.

At the wada Shakaram took out his bottle of medicines to take his dose. His friend saw this and said, "Here, you don't need medicines." His friend took the bottle from his hand and threw the medicines on the floor. Later they went for the *aarti*, Shakaram was impressed by the devotion, and love that the people had for Baba. After the aarti he sat in the Dwarkamai, against the pillar and gazed lovingly at Baba. A sense of calm and well-being enveloped him. He felt better than he had been in a long time. For the past month he was extremely nauseous and could not ingest even a bite of food. At night he felt as if his life itself was ebbing, and knew not what was happening to him.

According to his friend's wish he had come to Shirdi. Then it dawned on him, how healthy he became there. They stayed in Shirdi for a week. His nausea left, and to his surprise he started eating a whole *bhakar* of *jowari*. During their stay at Shirdi one of the days happened to be an *ekadasi*. His friend bought peru [guavas] for 'faral' [a meal of fruits]. Shakaram had wanted to eat guavas, but had refrained from doing so, as he feared a stomach upset. His friend made him eat them as prasad. To his surprise, nothing untoward happened. After taking permission from Baba, he and his friend returned to Kalyan and thence to Mumbai. This pilgrimage left a lasting impression on him. He was astounded by Baba's love and concern for His bhaktas. Then he composed an aarti and bhupali in praise of Baba's divinity, antarjnana and love.

[Ref : *Sai Leela*, Ank 4, Year 3,1925]

108

Leela 43: **Ramachandra Keshev Naik**

He was born in Pune. His father worked in the accounts section for the Military. At that time Swami Samarth of Akkalkot was well known and revered by a lot of people. His father was devoted to Swami Samarth. He would walk [Varkari] to Akkalkot with a group of devotees, just as Vitthal devotees did to Pandarpur. Whenever he made such pilgrimages he took Ramachandra with him. On many such trips he was accompanied by Swami Lakshman Pandit of Kamtipura and Nana Joshi Rakhe of Nagar. One day he received a telegram from Akkalkot stating that Swami Samarth is going to cast off his earthly body soon. So if he wanted to bid him farewell he should come soon.

Immediately his father left for Akkalkot taking Ramachandra with him. Nana Rakhe and Swami Pandit also accompanied them. At Akkalkot they had an audience with Swami Samarth, when Ramachandra's father said, "Maharaj, we will be destitute without you! Who will give refuge to me and my son?" Swami Samarth threw his padukas at him and said, "Keep worshipping these. In Ahmednagar jilha, in a village called Shirdi you will find my *avtar*. Bestow the love and affection you have for me on him. As you have been coming here so often go there likewise."

And so he did make a pilgrimage to Shirdi taking with him Ramachandra, Swami Lakshman Pandit and Nana Joshi. On the way they heard that the fakir at Shirdi was mad. And to top it all, He was a Muslim. Pandit and Rakhe could not bear the thought of bowing before a mad Muslim fakir. They said, "Since Swami Samarth has convinced you of the Fakir's divinity and avatarhood, you may bow before him, with devotion.

You may go there as often as you want. But we will not bow before a mad Muslim." All this had no effect on the father and son. Their faith was not shaken nor did they have any doubt.

On reaching Shirdi, they took Baba's darshan. How wonderful it was when the father and son saw Baba as Swami Samarth. Baba pointing to Rekhe and Pandit said, "They are high class, orthodox Brahmins!" Then pointing to the neem tree, He asked Ramachandra to pluck some branches and bring them. On doing so He divided the branches and asked them to eat the leaves. The leaves that Rekhe and Pandit got were extremely bitter, so bitter were they that they felt like throwing them.

On the other hand the leaves that Ramachandra and his father got were so sweet that they made a meal of them. Then drank water and belched with satisfaction. His friends were very sad about this incident. But Ramachandra's father had further proof that Baba was none other than Swami Samarth. He related a leela how Swami Samarth made half the branches of the neem tree sweet at Akkalkot. There is also a neem tree at Gangapur that has sweet leaves, this leela occurred to put a doubting devotee on the right path. Nonetheless it was proof for Ramachandra's father that Baba and Swami Samarth were one and the same.

The leela that Baba gave darshan as Swami Samarth was further strengthened when he saw two photographs of Baba in which Baba looks like Swami Samarth. Then he got another photograph. So he took the three photographs and got them all framed together. So sure is he of the likeness that He invites anyone who wants to see them to come to his home. The address given is Motiwala Jain, Block 11, Near Tad Dev Bridge, which is to the left of the stairs at Tad Dev, Grant Road Post Office, Mumbai.

Ramachandra and his father continued going to Shirdi. Once it so happened that he visited the home of Ganpat Krishnaji. As luck would have it Anandnath Maharaj was there. He was a renowned Gowd Brahmin from Vengule. He had totally devoted his life to Swami Samarth. He composed and sang *bhajans* of Swami Samarth. Hearing about Baba he had gone to pay his respects to Him. He told his devotees seated before him "Those who think or call Baba a mad Muslim, are in fact mad themselves. For they know not what is good and beneficial for them. Anyone who is interested in progressing spiritually should seek refuge at Baba's feet. For Baba is none other than God Himself." Hearing these words coming from Anand Nath Maharaja's mouth, father and son were filled with joy. Thenceforth whenever they went to Akkalkot they first visited Shirdi. [Ref: *Sai Leela,* Ank 4, Year 3, 1925]

Leela 44:   **Nangin Das Motilal**

Baba Che magazine (B.V. Deo) had some difficulty with the *Sai Leela* magazine issue, *Ank 11.* He therefore went to the beachfront bungalow of Nangin Das of Thana. Nangin Das was an affluent philanthropist. The reason for the visit was to ask him if he had any leelas to relate, so that they could be published in the '*Maharajache Anubhav*' section.

Nangin Das related the following leelas. His father had a burning desire to visit Shirdi and take Baba's darshan. Unfortunately it did not come to fruition and he passed away. One day he called Nangin Das and said, "I could not fulfill my desire to seek refuge at Baba's feet, but I sincerely hope you will go and meet Maharaj." Nangin Das had heard wonderful leelas of Baba. But it took him a long time to visit Shirdi.

One day he heard that two lawyer friends of his were going to Shirdi. They were Shingne of Mumbai and Ganga Das of Thana. He asked whether he could accompany them and they readily agreed. So they decided on the train they would take, and made all the arrangements. In the meantime he cancelled his plans. By nightfall, he had an irresistible urge to accompany them because he knew the train that they were to catch. He went to the station on time and met them. Three of them proceeded to Shirdi. On reaching Shirdi he felt that after coming from so far he should offer fifteen rupees as dakshina.

He consulted his friends about the amount to be offered. Simultaneously they answered one rupee. Nangin Das however felt it was not right to offer only one rupee. Since they had come as a group, he felt, he alone could not offer fifteen rupees. He was in a dilemma; he resolved it by taking with him five rupees as dakshina, though his heart was set on giving fifteen rupees.

The trio went for Darshan, and stood before Baba. Looking at Nangin Das Baba said "The 'Mahatara' (old man) could not come here, right. It is good that the son has come." They prostrated at Baba's feet and offered the dakshina. The other two gave a rupee each while Nangin Das gave five rupees. Baba looked at Nangin Das and said, "Give more dakshina. Give what you have decided in your mind. Give Me just that much." Happily he replied that he would go to the wada and send the dakshina. Nangin Das had already offered five rupees, so the balance was ten rupees. But as it was an even number and even numbers are considered inauspicious especially because it had a zero. So he sent eleven rupees. Seeing this, Maharaj said, "Give what you had in mind! Why give more"? Baba kept ten rupees and sent back one rupee. This rupee Nangin Das treasured.   [Ref: *Sai leela,* Ank 11, Year 2, 1924]

Leela 45: **Householder and His Younger Brother**

B.V. Deo states that at Thana, there lived a householder, who was devoted to Kaka Puranik. So also was his younger brother. In fact, both were very eager to meet Saints, and have *satsang* with them. [Unfortunately their names are not given] Pir Wadi was a small town near Satara where a famous saint named, Kondiba Maharaj lived. The older brother would sometime go to Pir Wadi, and sometime Maharaj would come to Thana. In 1911, two of his friends named Master and Joshi wanted to go to Shirdi. The two brothers were to accompany them. In December of that year they decided on a date, for the pilgrimage and made all arrangements. But on the day of departure the younger brother could not go for some reason. Thoroughly disappointed and sad, he said, "You go for if I am to have darshan of Baba it will happen here itself." The group proceeded to Shirdi each taking a coconut as offering for Baba. However the elder brother took two coconuts, one for himself and the other for his younger brother.

They took Baba's darshan, each offering his coconut and dakshina, at Baba's feet. Baba broke the coconut, kept one half, and returned the other to the rightful owner. The householder also offered the coconuts. Baba returned one half to him, and looking directly at him kept the other coconut. He said, " Has everyone got the other half." The householder understood that Baba had kept his brother's coconut for Himself and was very happy.

The next day the group went for darshan. At that time Baba was sitting with one leg outstretched and the other bent.

So he could not bow at both His feet. He thought, "I will do Namaskar only after Baba stretches both feet. Till such time I will sit and wait." He knelt before Baba and waited. After some time Baba stretched both His feet. Joyously the householder placed his head on Baba's feet. As he did so Baba took the cap from his head and threw it away. Baba then asked him to bring some udi. Having done so he handed the udi to Baba, who placed one hand on his head and with the other applied Udi on his forehead with His thumb. This gesture threw him into ecstasy.

He would bow at Baba's feet in the morning and evening. This made him extremely happy. If by chance he forgot to bow he became very restless and waited for a chance to do so. He had heard that Baba does not readily give permission to leave. And he had to go, as there was some problem at home. So he went to ask for his permission. At that time Baba had returned from Lendi Baugh. Baba was standing near the wall with His hand on it. As the householder approached Baba, he started shouting abuses. But as he went forward Baba said, "For so many days you have been prostrating before the Brahmin. Now he is dead. They killed him. Now you have come to prostrate before a Musalman [Muslim]." At once the householder realised that Kaka Puranic and Baba were one and the same.

Later Maharaj gave him permission to leave. The householder said, "Baba my younger brother was very eager to have Your darshan. When and how will he get Your Darshan" Baba answered, " It will happen, now go." Some time later a Konkani devotee with his family went to Shirdi for Baba's darshan. When it was time to leave he took Baba's permission. Baba granted the permission and said, "Will you do some work for Me?" The devotee readily agreed. Then Baba took some udi and made a packet and handed it to him saying, "If you go now you will catch the mail. When you board that train, between Kalyan and Mumbai a man will enter your compartment .He will ask you for a span of place to sit. Give that person this packet." The devotee said, "If such a person does not come to me. I will write, and tell You about it." Baba said "All right write to me."

And so it came to pass. The devotee reached Kopergaon, and found that there was no train going to Mumbai except the Mail. He and his family boarded the train and found two berths and were comfortable. The next morning they reached Kalyan. The compartment was by then crowded to suffocation. Eagerly he looked out for the person. But no one came and asked him for a span of place. After waiting at the station the Mail started proceeding towards Mumbai. What the Konkani devotee did not know was that the train halted at Thana, a station just before Mumbai. He thought that he should write to Baba and was about to do so when the train halted at Thana.

At Thana the younger brother had gone to meet his brother on the way to work. As he was delayed and late for work he ran to the station, and quickly boarded the waiting train. The compartment that he entered was the one in which the Konkani devotee sat. That compartment was over crowded. He looked around for some place and then he noticed the Konkani family. They were sitting comfortably on two berths. The little boy was sleeping next to his father. Between them was a span of place. The younger brother asked the Konkani gentleman, "Will you give me a span of place to sit as I feel I am going to faint." Hearing this the Konkani devotee remembered Baba's words. He readily picked up his son and made place for him near the window. Then he handed the packet of udi that Baba had given him and told him the whole story. The younger brother's joy knew no bounds. He took the packet and touched it to his forehead. His eyes filled with tears of joy for he felt that he had Baba's darshan right there [The householder, and his younger brother requested BV Deo not to mention their names; hence they are referred to as the householder and the younger brother]. [Ref: *Sai Leela*, Ank 11, Year 2, 1924]

Leela 46: **Tumache Me Bhar**
Vahine Sarvatha
[I will carry your burden]

Marthanda Mhalsapathy relates two leelas about Baba's intense love and caring for His bhaktas. In the *Shri Sai Satcharita*, Chapter 7 the leela of Baba taking upon Himself the bubonic plague of Balwant Khaparde is given.

Marthand's (Mhalsapathy son) mother had once gone to visit her brother, who lived in Nandur Singota. As usual Mhalsapathy was sitting close to Baba, and doing seva. Suddenly Baba said, "Arre one of My bhaktas has developed an abscess, and is in a great deal of distress. I too have developed an abscess on My buttock. Soon I will feel better." Mhalsapathy could clearly see that Baba had developed an abscess on His bottock. And was having a great deal of pain and discomfort in sitting. Mhalsapathy was very concerned about this. But Baba said, "Bhagat don't worry, after two or three days it will heal, and I will feel better". Mhalsapathy did not know at that time whose abscess Baba had taken upon Himself. Though he knew that Baba would readily take the illness of His bhaktas on Himself. And relieve them of their pain and suffering. Two days later the abscess did burst and Baba was relieved of the pain.

Three days after this incident Mhalsapathy received a letter from his wife. She wrote how she had developed an abscess on her buttock. As the pain was unbearable she prayed to Baba for relief. Immediately she got relief, and two days later the abscess burst and she felt all right. It was then that he realised that Baba had taken the abscess upon Himself, when

116

his wife prayed to Him for relief. Overwhelmed by Baba's love and compassion Mhalsapathy said, "Look Marthand to give your mother relief Baba took upon Himself the pain, and abscess. Hence your mother became all right. And our God and mother suffered so much."

[Ref: *Sai Leela*, Ank 4, Year 29, 1952]

Leela 47: "What a Great Mother You Are? Here Take Your Baby"

Baba rarely left Shirdi in His physical body. Sometimes He would go to Rahata or Nigog Neemgaon. There He would visit the home of Nana Sahib Dengle. Nana Sahib was affluent and owned vast acres of farmlands. Bapu Maali helped him with the working of the farm. Next to the pasture was a path that Baba used when He would come and go from Dengle's home.

This leela took place during the monsoons. Bapu Mali, along with ten to fifteen people went to the pasture to cut grass. Near the pasture there was a tamarind tree and next to it was a 'Kaut' [wood Apple] tree. One of the female workers laid her child under the tamarind tree. The tree was huge and provided shade. Often people sat and had their lunch there. Making the child comfortable she preceded to meaw the grass. A short while later there was a passing storm. It became gusty and torrents of rain fell. Everyone ran for cover and took shelter in an abandoned hut nearby. The mother ran with the rest of the labourers having forgotten that she had placed her child under the tree. After quite sometime she remembered her child. Panic stricken, she ran crying loudly, and calling the child's name. At that time the rain had lessened a bit.

But there were puddles everywhere. She jumped over some and waded through the others to reach her child. Bapu along with some other labourers ran after her. They reached the tamarind tree and what they saw sent waves of wonder over them. Under the tree stood Baba who had the infant cradled in His arms. Recognising the mother Baba shouted, "Avo rande! [an abuse]. What a great mother you are? Here take your Baby" The mother took her child in her arms, and looked at him in wonder. As the child was absolutely dry. She then looked around and saw rain pouring down through the branches of the tree. Huge puddles were under the tree. Only Baba and her child were dry and Baba was standing on a small area of dry earth. Bapu Maali and the labourers looked carefully and saw the same thing. It dawned on them that Baba had materialised there to save her baby.

The kaut tree died some years later, but the tamarind tree still stands, for Baba sanctified it by standing underneath it.

[Ref: *Sai Leela*, Ank 4, Year 29,1952]

Leela 48: **Kashinath Shankar Dubey**
and Raghunath Dubey

Kashinath lived with his family in Ganesh Peth, Pune. In the year 1913 or 1914 an epidemic of plague broke out there. People in and around the city fled, abandoning their homes and belongings. Kashinath however did not leave his home. He had faith in Baba and knew that Baba would protect him. But he asked his son Raghunath to take his family to his in-laws home. Raghunath before leaving Pune mentally decided to have Baba's darshan at Shirdi. Preoccupied as he was with packing, and taking a long journey with his young child and wife, he forgot to go to Shirdi.

He travelled by train and everything was all right till Dhond station. His younger son who was perfectly healthy, suddenly became seriously ill and was dying. Upset as he was with the condition of his son, his wife also started running a high fever. By evening the fever was very high and she showed signs of plague. Finally he reached Navalgudas, his wife's village. But his problems did not end here. In that village he knew no body, nor could he speak Kannada the language spoken there. At first he could not find a doctor. Then a kind gentleman seeing his plight befriended him. He brought a famous doctor with him to treat his wife. The doctor seeing the condition of his wife gave up hope of her surviving. He would not treat her as she was six months pregnant.

Raghunath being the oldest member in that house all the responsibility fell on his shoulders. The condition of his wife, started worsening and the fever started increasing with each passing hour. Totally disheartened and helpless, he cried to Baba for help. With complete concentration and faith he laid his problems at Baba's feet. That very day, at 4 p.m. Baba gave him *shakshatkar.* He entered his home through the northern door, and sat on a *chowrang* [small stool usually used for pujas]. He looked at his wife with compassion and kindness. Then He took some *teerth* from a *kamandalu* [brass vessel used by ascetics] and made her drink it. Following this He passed His hands over her body. From the pocket of His kafni, He took some udi and applied it on her forehead and her body and said, "Prayaschit aashe Bole laya pramane karave. Naa kaleyas thayanche bhogave laagthe" [What you say you must do. If you do not you have to repent, and suffer like this]. As Baba was saying this, some children were making a noise behind him, this distracted Raghunath. He turned to see what the noise was about and in the meantime Baba disappeared.

The whole scenario left Raghunath dumbfounded with awe that he could not understand what happened. But when he looked at his wife he saw the mark of udi on her forehead. This convinced him that Baba did come to his home for their welfare. At about 9 o'clock that night the fever started falling, and the next day his wife was well enough to make a meal. Some time later they did make the pilgrimage to Shirdi. Baba told this story to everyone. [Ref: *Sai Leela*, Ank 11, 1924]

Leela 49: Eka Sai Bhakta Kadun [From a Sai Bhakta]

It was in the year 1917 that he went to Shirdi for Baba's darshan [This Sai bhakta wants to remain anonymous]. This pilgrimage was because he had heard of the divinity and glory of Baba from so many friends and acquaintances. He was very eager to have Baba's darshan. Although he intended to go as soon as possible, he was quite confused. Because he did not know where Shirdi was. His mind was in turmoil. "Where was Shirdi? How do I get there? What transportation will take me there? I know no one in Shirdi?" he thought.

Fifteen days before his date of departure, His seven month old son died of fever. This saddened his heart greatly and made him even more anxious to seek refuge in Baba. " When will I have Baba's darshan?" This thought kept repeating itself in his mind. That night he had a vivid dream, in which he saw five Satpurushas and amongst them was Baba. They were seated in a place that looked like a masjid. At that time he did not know that was the Dwarkamai. In front of them he saw heaps of ashes [*udi*]. He asked a man next to him, "Who is Baba?" The man pointed his finger towards Him. He ran and fell at Baba's feet. Just then he awoke and there ended the dream.

Following that dream, everything fell in place. Five days later the problem he had of getting the necessary funds for the pilgrimage resolved itself. A man from his neighbourhood came to him and asked him whether he would accompany him to Shirdi. They both set out and the neighbour took care of everything. On reaching Shirdi they went for darshan. He had mentally decided to give one rupee as dakshina. He had darshan and Baba asked him for one rupee as dakshina. Then he sat down, Baba looked at him and said, "Dhuk karaaya che karan kay? Mane mulga gayala, Malaa he ek divshe dhey teva vyaca aahe. Mrythulokath aalyaver mrythuha aaj naahe udya yenaarch" [Roughly Translated – "What is the reason for your sorrow? Your son has gone; I have to leave this body one day. If you come to this earth death will surely come. If not today, it will certainly come tomorrow."].

Greatly comforted by Baba's words he stayed at Shirdi for four days. He asked Baba for the permission to leave and it was easily granted. At Kopergaon station he learned that the train was delayed by an hour due to an accident at the preceding station. Because of this delay, he would not be able to catch the connecting Mail to Mumbai. But this thought did not bother him, as he was sure that Baba would look after him. He boarded the train and reached Manmad, there he learned the Mail was also delayed by an hour. This delay was due to an accident enroute. So he reached Mumbai safely. As time went by, his financial condition improved. He felt that it was because of Baba's grace.

His *ishtadev* was Shankar and daily he would perform *maanas puja* [mental adoration]. After his pilgrimage to Shirdi whenever he did this he saw Baba seated on top of the *Shivling*.   [Ref: *Sai Leela*, Ank 13, Year 1926]

Leela 50: **Mrs Jog and the Buffalo**

Baba loved and respected Tai Jog [Mrs Jog] very much. He lovingly called her *aaye* (mother). She was devoted to Him, and made whatever *prasad* He wanted and looked after the devotees that He sent to stay with her with great care.

One day when she took the **breakfast prasad** to the Dwarkamai, Baba called her and said, " Aaye today a Buffalo will come to you. So make a lot of *puran poles* [a chappati filled with cooked *daal* and jaggary and cardamum]. Top it with a lot of ghee [clarified butter] and give it to the buffalo to eat." Aaye readily agreed to do so. But she said, "Baba I will surely make a whole lot of puran poles with a lot of *ghee* (clarified butter). I will feed the buffalo, but where am I to go and search for this buffalo. And how am I going to recognise him?" Baba replied, "Aaye why do you worry about this? As soon as you finish preparing the puran poles the buffalo will come to your door." In dismay Aaye replied, " Baba the house that I live in has two doors. Everyday a whole lot of buffalo's pass that way on their way to graze. Often they stop at my door for food that I may give." Baba explained, "Aaye as soon as you have prepared the puran poles and applied ghee this particular buffalo will come to the rear door and wait."

Satisfied with Baba's answer Aaye went home. With great care she made a lot of delicious puran poles. Making sure that they were laden with ghee. It was about 12:30 when she went to the rear door and found the buffalo waiting.

She was surprised, but happy, that Baba's words were true. Then she returned with a whole lot of puran poles and fed the buffalo. The buffalo ate all the poles, and then died right in front of her. Aaye was frightened, distraught and sad at the turn of events. Aaye felt that she was responsible for the death of the buffalo. She went inside and carefully examined each and every ingredient that she had used, but could not find anything wrong. Her mind was in turmoil. She said, "I made the puran poles, with love, and happiness. Then how did this happen? Why did this buffalo die? Though I did not kill him, everyone will hold me responsible for the death. What will everyone think and say about me. I just followed Baba's orders. Whose buffalo was it anyway? When the owner comes to know about this he will say I killed the buffalo. If the owner asks for payment, how much must that buffalo have cost? What if he registers a complaint? What will be its outcome?. Baba is the creator of this cosmos, I followed His instructions, so if the outcome is bad He will forgive me for it." Thinking like that she pacified herself.

She went to Baba and told Him in detail what happened. Baba said, "Aaye do not be afraid. What happened is not bad it had to happen anyway. That buffalo had only this desire [*vaasana*] left. Once that desire was satisfied he got free from that womb. Now he will get a good rebirth. Now you go home with out fear. Don't feel bad or sad as you have freed him from a lower birth. When you have freed him from the rebirth of a buffalo and given him a chance for a better birth then why should you be unhappy?" With these words Baba comforted her and she went home happily.

[Ref: *Sai Leela*, Ank 11 and 12, Year 4, 1926]

Leela 51:   **Jog and Ganga Snaan**

Baba often said, "Pude leye changle divese yethele" [Roughly Translated – Very good days will come in the future] this leela is written by Mahatara. He tells the leela of Naga Mahasheya's father who wanted to have a bath in the Bhagirithi river. The reason for this was that it was *parvani* [A shub kaal or auspicious time] and traditionally everyone went to have a dip in a holy river. He pestered his son to take him to the Bhagirithi, but his son said, " We will see". Utterly disappointed with his son, the father accepted his fate. Little did he know that at the exact muhurath, there was a break in the wall, and the river with all its force flooded the land. Hence, his father and all the villagers had a bath in the Bhagirithi.

Many decades later this same *parvani* [auspicious time] came and Bapu Sahib Jog and his wife wanted to have a bath in Ganga at Kopergaon. Baba called the Godavari river Ganga. Hence the rest of the devotees did the same.

Jog went to take permission from Baba who said, "Bapu Sahib! Baghu thyacha vichar udhya sakali" [Roughly Translated – "Bapu Sahib look we will think about it tomorrow"]. Bapu Sahib replied "Baba the auspicious time is at seven in the morning. We will have to get up at about four in the morning to reach Kopergaon.

Only then will it be possible to have a dip in the Ganga." Again Baba repeated the same words. Jog pleaded with Baba many times in various ways. But Baba had only one reply, "We will see tomorrow." Jog and his wife were quite disappointed, as such a *shub kaal* came only once in a lifetime.

Bapu Sahib was such a staunch devotee that he would not go against Baba's wish. That night he was very restless, and it was the night that Baba slept in the *chavdi*. In the morning he performed *kakad aarti*, and had just finished the ritual when the villagers came running. They were shouting that the canals were filling up with water from the Ganga. Baba looking at Jog said, "Tu sagli rath leye shive dileyas, pan Devache daya, Ganga aaplapashi aale. Jaa atha angole karun gheye." [Roughly Translated – "The whole night you hurled abuses at Me. But due to God's kindness the Ganga has come to us. Now go and have dip in it"]. Thus Bapu Sahib, his wife and the rest of the villagers had a dip in the Ganga.

The canal that was to supply Shirdi with water from the Godavari was not completed at that time. There were yet two to four months for the water to be released into it. So much water flooded Shirdi that no one could have dreamt of. The reason being that a dam further up had broken. It was then declared useless and from another dam water was given to Shirdi. Because of the abundant water, Bapu Sahib had a bath in the morning and noon. Seeing his delight Baba said, "Arre Bapu Sahib see how kind God is. But we do not place total faith in Him nor do we have 'Saburi.'" The author heard Baba use the word 'Saburi' a lot. He says, 'Saburi' means unfailing, concentrated faith.

In the September of 1910 Mahatara first went to Shirdi. At that time the water for the village was being drawn from the wells. He remembers Baba saying, "Arre Ganga aaplya paya pashi ye ele" [Roughly Translated – "Arre the Ganga will be at our feet"].

At that time it seemed an impossibility. After many years the Survey Department sought permission and the government approved of the plan of letting the water from the Godavari flow into Shirdi. Kopergaon is about eight miles from Shirdi and much of the land was barren. But now the lands on the way to Kopergaon are lush farmlands. In fact, there are canals in and around Shirdi that supply water to the village from the Godavari.   [Ref: *Sai Leela*, Ank 4-5, Year 6, 1928]

Leela 52: **Vitthal Darshan**

Mahatara [Tarkhad] had a dear friend who with his wife, son and daughter-in-law went to Pandarpur [Though, Tarkhad writes that it was a friend of his, I firmly believe the experience, happened to him and his family. Besides no name is mentioned]. His wife was about 57-year-old. She was in good health, had good eyesight, but was rather short. They went up to the idol for darshan. Her son led the group, he went and placed his head on the feet of the Lord and moved away. Next his mother paid obeisance, placing her head on the Lord's feet. After doing so she called out to her son and said, "Arre! How soft and warm the feet of the Lord are?" Her son responded saying, "Yes", for he had the same experience. The daughter-in-law also experienced the same thing. Three of them were overwhelmed by the experience.

Mrs Tarkhad was devoted to Baba. The family performed *puja* daily. Being a spiritual person Mrs Tarkhad, read a lot of scriptures and religious books. Therein she advised people to make pilgrimage to Pandarpur at least once in their lifetime, as it was a means to attain salvation. She told Jyotindra about this and expressed her desire to make the pilgrimage. Jyotindra however told her to ask Baba and seek His approval.

On her next visit to Shirdi, she asked Baba to permit her to go to Pandarpur. Baba replied, "Arre Aaye! For us Shirdi is everything and there is no need to go here and there." She was rather disappointed. Nonetheless she continued telling Baba that pilgrims visiting Pandarpur firmly believe that Vitthal was present there. And once you have darshan, then the path to salvation is easy. She expressed her desire to make that pilgrimage and perform puja at least once in her life. Baba knew that she was devoted to Vitthal and genuinely wanted to make the pilgrimage. He said, "Aaye do not worry you will visit Pandarpur and fulfill your desire." On reaching home she informed Baba Sahib of Baba's approval. After making all arrangements, Jyotindra and she proceeded to Pandarpur.

They took a bath, had breakfast and after the morning rush was over they walked to the temple. Mrs Tarkhad had brought all the *puja* material with her. They entered the Sanctum Sanctorum and sought permission from the priest to perform the puja. With great devotion she performed the puja. Then at the end of the puja she wanted to garland the deity. But the priest refused as no one was permitted to climb the dais on which the *murthi* (idol) stood. Sadly she told Jyotindra that her puja would be incomplete. As usual Jyotindra said that she should seek Baba's help as He had granted permission. She closed her eyes in prayer and asked Vitthal to accept her garland.

And Lo! she beheld the murthi slide down from the dais ready to be garlanded. Jyotindra saw this and shook her and asked her to see for herself that the Lord had responded to her prayers. Happily she placed the garland around His neck and the Lord was back on the dais. The priest was a witness to this; he jumped down from the dais and fell at their feet. Jyotindra told him that they were devoted to Baba and He had granted them permission to go to Pandarpur.

When she visited Shirdi later, Baba asked her pointedly "Aaye did you meet Vithoba?". With tears of joy in her eyes she replied, "Baba this is all your leela. I am now ready to depart from this world. As I now consider my life complete." She thanked Baba profusely for the wonderful experience.

[Ref: Sai Leela, Ank 4-5, Year 6, 1928]

Leela 53: **Shankar Rao Gavankar and Lala Lakhmichand**

In 1907, Shankar Rao developed an irresistible desire to have *darshan* of various saints. He started reading about their lives, listened to *bhajans* and discourses. He met Narayan Maharaj of Khedgaon, who was visiting Mulund in Thane jilha. Some days later he heard the *kirtans* of Das Ganu Maharaj in the home of Govindrao Dabolkar. He found that the saints of that time were very much like the ancient Saints. And he got wonderful experiences. Following this his desire to meet saints increased manifold and he met them without any effort on his part. Often some friend would ask him to join him on a pilgrimage, and there he would meet a saint.

At that time he was at Vasai where he worked in the Vasai Court. One day he received a letter from Lala Madan Gopal, a friend of his. His friend resided at Shimla, and worked for the Government Railway Board. He asked Shankar Rao to accompany him to Khedgaon, for darshan of Narayan Maharaj. Lala had made arrangements for his stay at Kalyan, where they would meet when he arrived from Shimla. Shankar Rao took leave for a week, packed his bags and set out. But first he alighted at Vile Parle and went to his brother's home. There he learned that Lala had sent a telegram, stating that due to unavoidable circumstances he was unable to come. And his brother should tell Shankar Rao this. Now he was in Vile Parle with a week's leave, he was wondering whether he should spend it there or shorten it. That very evening his friend Lala Lakhmichand visited him and asked him to accompany him to Shirdi.

Lakhmichand was looking for a companion who was compatible and shared his views and beliefs, and they both decided to go. Shankar Rao thought that he had a weeks' leave and instead of spending it there, he would go to Shirdi. Since it was the first visit to Shirdi for both of them, they tried to gather as much information as they could. They wanted to know how to get there? From the place of arrival how far was Shirdi? The cost involved the fares and such things? They had heard rumours that Baba beat first time visitors. Finally Bahu Sahib gave them correct and useful information.

Bahu Sahib gave them a basket of fruit and flowers to offer to Baba. While Raghunath Wagh gave a garland and Khanaya Lal gave them four *annas* and asked them to buy *Perus* [guavas] as Baba was very fond of them. They alighted at Dadar and caught the connecting train to Manmad. To their delight Nana Sahib got into the same compartment on his way home. He saw their entire luggage and advised them to leave some behind, which he would take to Kalyan with him and they could retrieve it on their return journey. He also asked them to convey his namaskars to Baba.

As both of them loved to do bhajans, they did so all the way to Nasik. At midnight a Muslim got into their compartment. He too was on his way to Shirdi, so they asked him about Baba. He told them that Baba was a great *Awalia*. At 6 o'clock the next morning they got down at Kopergaon. There was not a single *tonga* at the station. At that very moment a tonga drew up and the driver said that Bahu Sahib had sent him. The luggage was loaded on the tonga, and the two of them rested for about two hours. After a bath and breakfast they proceeded to Shirdi. For the next ten to fifteen minutes the horses did not run or even walk swiftly. They were well built, and even the master's whip did not induce them to run. Just then a women carrying a basket of guavas ran up to them and said, "Dada you wanted to buy perus, here buy whatever you want and give the rest to Baba from me." This reminded Shankar Rao of his promise to Khanaya Lal.

At that time he did not know that the perus from the banks of the Godavari were fresh, delectable and famous. He thought that he would buy them at Shirdi. No sooner had he bought the perus, the horses ran well and did not stop till they reached Shirdi. The leela given above is described in *Shri Sai Satcharita,* Chapter 28. Here Shankar Rao writes a detailed account.

They alighted at Sathe wada. At that time there were about hundred and fifty pilgrims present there. They met Nulkar and his friend Neelkant, who welcomed them with a cup of tea. Shankar Rao inquired as to how they should go for Baba's darshan? On reaching the Dwarkamai they found Baba shouting abuses at the people seated there. Baba was alone except for a Deshat brahmin who was there, and he was pressing Baba's back. The rest of the devotees had fled to the Sabha Mandap. Seeing Shankar Rao and Lakhmichand about to enter the Sanctum Sanctorum, the devotees told them not to enter as Baba was in a rage. And asked them to sit in the Sabha Mandap. Shankar Rao did not pay any attention to what they said and he climbed the steps. There he stood for a minute or so. Although Baba was shouting he did not hear what He said. Then he heard Baba say, "Jao idher say" [Go away from here]. So he turned back, and sat against the wall of the masjid. His mind was quite confused and perturbed and he said to himself, "Until Baba summons me I will not go." However the first impression that he got upon seeing Baba was that He looked like, Swami Samarath of Akkalkot. Nonetheless he felt that Baba, the Sadguru had motherly love for him. Within a minute or two, Baba sent a person to call them. Both of them went into the Sanctum Sanctorum and sat at Baba's feet. Meanwhile the rest of the devotees seized the moment and went into the Sanctum Sanctorum. They offered the perus, the garland, the fruits and prostrated. Then they did the ritualistic puja. Baba got someone to distribute the perus as prasad. Then He took one peru and breaking it into two halves gave them to Lakhmichand and Shankar Rao. Applying udi He said, "Khana khao aur Wada Mai aaram karo" [Have your meals and rest in the Wada].

For the next two to three days, they stayed in the wada, and did not spend much time in the Dwarkamai. However, they had the darshan of Baba in the morning, and then again when He passed by the wada on His way to Lendi Baugh. After two days the devotees that had come from Mumbai left. Thus there were only the four of them – Shankar Rao, Lakhmichand and Nulkar, who stayed there with his friend Neelkant permanently. "After coming to Shirdi there is a profound change in me," said Neelkant to Shankar Rao. Strange and unusual thoughts kept arising in Shankar Rao's mind. "If Baba is a Satpurush, then why does He shout abuses at people? Why does He have so much of anger, and fly into a rage? How will such behaviour help the people? Will this behaviour benefit the world, or the country? If He does not give any 'Updesh' I have come here needlessly. So why should I stay here? All he ever says is "Khana Khao Aur Aaram Karo"! [Eat and rest] Other than this He says nothing." These thoughts stayed with him for the next two days or so.

The next day, at about 8 a.m. when he was having breakfast and was talking to Nulkar he got the overpowering aroma of incense. He knew that Nulkar had not burnt incense. Then where was it coming from? He went to investigate and followed the aroma, only to find that it was coming from the Dwarkamai. But no one had burnt incense there. Then he realised that it was Baba's way of bringing him to the Dwarkamai. Shankar Rao and Lakhmichand entered the Sanctum Sanctorum, and according to Baba's wish sat on either side of Baba's outstretched legs. Shankar Rao sat to the right and Lakhmichand to the left, and started massaging Baba's legs. Then Baba asked a devotee to bring His chillum. Baba took a puff and gave it to Shankar Rao, and then He took another puff and handed it to Lakhmichand. This He did thrice, Lakhmichand took a puff or two, but when it was handed to Shankar Rao, he did not smoke it, but just held it in his hand. At that time his mind was crowded with thoughts, and they were " may be Baba handed the chillum to me to hold it as He wanted some rest? I'm not of the same spiritual status, so he won't do that, it will be an insult if I smoke the same Chillum?" At that very moment Baba said, "Smoke" and handed the chillum to him. Then he took a puff, then again and again he smoked it. While this was taking place Baba was saying something. Soon he realised that Baba was relating incidents of their past.

Baba related with dates his family history right from his grandfather's time. Some of the incidents Shankar Rao knew, the rest he confirmed when he returned home. Baba told him how his grandfather's Guru stayed with them for twelve years. This is what He said, "My Father and Mother were there. For twelve years I stayed with them. They looked after me very well. Many people, relatives and friends said unpleasant things and gave them a lot of trouble. But did they lose anything? Did they have dearth of anything because of this? Allah looks at those who troubled them! Look! If you live properly and do good Allaha will do good! But if you do bad Allah will do bad. I am at Gangapur, at Pandarpur. In fact, I am everywhere. I am in the whole world and the whole world is in Me! What you are holding at present do not leave. In two or four days you will find Allaha." After Baba narrated this He took quite a quantity of udi and applied it to his whole face And said, "Have your meals and take rest"! Taking some khobra [desiccated coconut] He gave it as prasad and asked them to go and have lunch. That was the day of their departure. After lunch they went and got permission to leave. Since he had run out of money, Shankar Rao borrowed five rupees from Nulkar. But after paying their dues he was left with only one and a half rupee. He felt embarrassed to ask Nulkar for more money. There was no way he could reach Vasai the next day on that amount. He had to join duty the next day at 11 a.m. By then it was 2 o'clock and there was no tonga, and no money and Baba had granted permission to go. He decided to go and see Baba once more as a parting salutation. He took a coconut and went to the Dwarkamai. Baba had just finished His lunch. Looking at him Baba said, "You have to join duty tomorrow, if you leave right now you will be able to catch the train."

Just then a friend of his arrived from Indore [His name is not mentioned] Baba asked him to accompany them. The Indore friend had stopped on his way to Mumbai for darshan. He had hired a tonga to and from Shirdi. Thus Shankar Rao and Lakhmichand were able to go with him. On reaching Kopergaon station they found that they had missed the train. The next train was at 8 p.m. The Indore friend purchased tickets for it. They reached Manmad only to find that the connecting train was delayed by three hours due a derailment. The next day they were still enroute. At 11 a.m. he had to join duty. After all these mishaps they reached Mumbai at 3 p.m. Lakhmichand joined duty that day, but Shankar Rao did not. He accepted the hospitality of his friend and went to his home in Sion. The result was that he still had one and a half rupee left as his friend took care of all expenses enroute. This friend belonged to the famous Dalvi family and had a good job in the customs department. Shankar Rao had met his friend after many years. Both had studied at Elphenston High School.

That evening he met a colleague from work who told him that a person at work was maligning him, by telling his supervisor that he was irresponsible and had overstayed his leave. But this did not make him anxious. He went to work the next day, only to find that his mother-in-law was in the chamber. He met his senior officer who asked the reason for his overstaying the leave. He truthfully told all that had happened. Satisfied with his explanation the officer, who knew him well signed his application for extension of leave for a day. Seeing how easily he was granted leave his mother-in-law was embarrassed.

Shankar Rao concludes this leela by saying that "Saints perform *chamatkars* [miracles] for various reasons sometimes to inculcate faith. At other times to put the person on the right path and sometimes for the spiritual upliftment of the devotee. But each devotee going to the saint must know in his heart the reason for the visit." [Ref: *Sai Leela*, Ank 12, Year 3, 1926]

Leela 54:   **Yoga and Siddhis**

Rama Chandra Atmaram Tarkhad was the editor of the *Sai Leela* magazine for many years. He wrote many articles on philosophy, religion, and the Occult under the Pen name Mahatara. For that was the name that Baba called him. Here he writes on yoga and *siddhis*. It is very insightful as it gives Baba's views on siddhis.

His friend [name not mentioned] first visited Shirdi in 1910, but he could not appreciate or comprehend Baba's leelas. He started reading the various books on the lives of saints. He read the life of Ram Krishna and Vivekananda. He liked the Vivekananda's book on "*Raj Yog*". As he was well versed in physiology and comparative anatomy he fully understood the yoga practices written therein. Then he decided to practise yoga seriously with the intent of attaining God rather than attaining the *siddhis* that came with it. Slowly he started the yoga and felt better, both physically and mentally. It was the 12th September 1912, when he returned home from work at about 7 p.m., had a cold-water bath and sat in a yoga posture. He started doing *pranayama*, and after a little while he saw a pink light. And no matter what he did, it would not disappear.

He got up and washed his face with cold water and sat down. Again the same light appeared only this time it was red. He repeatedly washed his face, but the same light was there. He then turned his eyes to another direction, and he saw a building on fire. He wondered whose it was when he realised that it was his mill that was on fire. He could see that the fire had devastated a part of the mill. Unable to bear it any longer, he stood before Baba's photograph and said, " Deva to attain You I started this pranayama and not to attain siddhis. From today I will stop this." This incident he told his family, when a Sepoy from the Mill told him about the fire. To which he replied, " I know" and went to the Mill. Thus the fire was extinguished.

About three months following this incident, Tarkhad, his friend and his wife went to Shirdi. They all went for darshan, and did *shashtang namaskar*. Baba looking at his friend said, "Kaya re, raand chitkayala pahath hothi? Aare Me kashi chitkun dhene! Aapalyala asha randoborobar kaahi kaarayava naahi" [Roughly Translated – "What has the prostitute [Baba means *siddhis* here] stuck on to you? Arre how will I let her stick onto you? We have nothing to do with this prostitute". Hearing this, his friend was relieved and very happy. But his wife could not understand the conversation. She had complete faith in her husband, but was very confused. Nonetheless these words were coming from Baba so they had to be true. Later he explained to her what Baba meant. His friend however continued to do pranayama, and with Baba's grace he got wonderful results.   [Ref: *Sai Leela*, Ank 4-5, Year 6, 1929]

135

Leela 55: **Goddess Annapurna in Shirdi**

Ramachandra A. Tarkhad, his family and his dear friend [name not mentioned] visited Shirdi on sixth of September 1910. The group consisted of about thirty people. They boarded the train at Dadar and reached Shirdi at about 10 a.m. His friend was very anxious to meet Baba, the reason being that he was a *Prathana Samajist* and did not believe in the worship of idols. Though he had read various religious books, he had a lot of doubts and was confused. About two months before this he had heard Das Ganu's *kirtan*, and it left an indelible impression on him. Hence, the burning desire to meet Baba.

When he beheld Baba's serene, divine and loving countenance he was overwhelmed. He said to himself, "You are a Satpurush, but I do not have the sense or knowledge to absorb this. As the others are offering incense, camphor and coconuts I am doing the same. And I hope that by doing so I am not being entrapped?" Just then Baba picked up a coconut and said, "Who's this?" His companions pointing to him said, "It is His." Baba holding the coconut said, "Take it." The friend got up to receive it when Baba said, "It takes a long time for this man to get up". Hearing this the rest of the group laughed heartily but this did not offend him. While he was receiving the prasad he said to himself, "Baba I don't understand anything. But henceforth I am going to place all my burden on You." Baba said, "All right". He felt that the others were spiritually advanced, but he was ignorant. However, he had a comfortable feeling that there was some one to support him Then he said, "Baba may I ask You a question?" Baba replied, " Ask". Then he said, "Baba do You look upon everybody

136

with the same equality of vision?" Baba replied, "You must have sense to ask this question. Of course, My grace is equally extended to every person. And I look upon everybody with the same equality of vision." Again the whole group laughed heartily. The friend was not offended by the laughter. Instead he felt immense hope and courage that Baba was behind him. Thinking along these lines his friend felt that he too should have an *ishtadev*, his personal God to meditate on and worship in his own personal way. At that very moment the *aarti* started. Everyone stood up, so did he. He looked around and saw the window of the old school was open and he could look outside. Every evening Radha Krishna Mai would light lamps and place them there. Through that window he could see an exquisitely beautiful and *tejasvi* [bright] lady. She was bedecked with jewellery from head to toe. Her clothes were of the finest silk and brocade.

Such ethereal beauty he had never seen before, nor would he ever see again in his life. She was looking at him intently. He responded with joy and wonder. Who could this beautiful lady be? How did she manage to have such extraordinary jewellery and beautiful clothes in this small village? How could she walk about without fear or worry? Where must she be keeping her jewellery? Many such questions kept propping up in his mind. Suddenly he realised that he was looking at someone's wife! He turned his gaze and looked at Baba, who was indeed looking at him in a knowing way. The *aarti* continued but his gaze kept returning to that ethereal beauty. Finally he made up his mind not to look that side and kept his resolve.

He visited Shirdi during the next few months and saw that lady again. One evening he was talking to Balaram Mankar when he mentioned that beautiful lady. Mankar told him that she was none other than Annapurna Maa. And he too was fortunate to have her *darshan*. Mankar said that following the *darshan*, he gave up the materialistic things of life and made Shirdi his home, and became a fakir. The friend did find a change in his life. Before he had an utter disdain for women, but now he respected them.

[Ref: Sai Leela, Ank 11, Year 2, 1924]

Leela 56: **Baba Goes Three Times a Day to Tarkhad's Home**

Mahatara writes this leela, it conveys the deep love and *rinanubandh* that Baba had for Tarkhad and their friend. In 1917, his friend stayed at Shirdi for Dussehra and Khojagiri Purnima and then returned to Mumbai. His manager wanted to meet Baba. So his friend, his wife and youngest son, returned to Shirdi [As their names are not mentioned, I will use the noun friend, wife and son, here and in future]. They stayed there for three days and then took permission to leave. While taking leave Friend cried inconsolably, he just couldn't stop his tears. He could not bear the thought of leaving Baba. Little did he know that the next Dusshera Baba would take Mahasamadhi?. Baba in His characteristic way said, "Aasa kaya re yadyapani karthose? Me thikde thujayapashi naahi ka?" [Roughly Translated – "Why are you behaving in this mad fashion? Am I not with you there?"]. To which friend answered, "Intellectually I can understand this but I have no experience." Who else but Baba can give such an assurance and his friend lived his life on this assurance.

Around 1915 Friend, Wife, and Son had gone to Shirdi; they spent some peaceful time there. One day they were sitting in the Dwarkamai when Baba said, "Aaye I have to go to your home three times a day. Wife replied, "Yes Baba". At that time there was a lady from Shirdi who said, "Baba You say strange things. You say You go thrice a day to this lady's home. Yet I

138

see You sitting here all the time." Baba replied, "I do not speak untruth. I am Maha Lakshmi. Aaye don't I come to your house? And you give lunch and delicious savouries to eat." Again she replied, "Yes Baba". The lady turned to Wife and asked her if this was true. And Wife replied in the affirmative. Baba then asked the Son "Don't I come to your home every day?" The Son replied, "Yes". Baba looking at him said, " I go from here and take the straight road. Just before his home there is a wall I jump over it. The railway tracks are to be crossed. Only then do I see Bhau's home. Isn't that so?"

Now the son was confused. He said, "No Baba first our home then the railway tracks". Baba insisted that He crossed the tracks first then reached his home. The Son was confused for a while. Then he remembered that daily he and his mother would offer whatever they ate, drank as *naivedya* to Baba. Their front door faced east, they had to come out of that door and facing west they offered it. West because Shirdi was west of Mumbai and only after the offering was made did they eat the food. They considered it to be Baba's prasad. When there was such love and devotion Baba had to go there and accept it.   [Ref: *Sai Leela*, Ank 6-7, Year 6,1929]

Leela 57: **Babancha Hemard Offers Paan Vida to Baba**

On 15th September, Hemard Panth had a vivid dream at 4 a.m. in the morning. Swami Vimalanand of the Damboli appeared and gave him a silver rupee along with two silver four *anna* coins and said, "Tomorrow at twelve noon you must offer me, hundred tender 'Paan' [beetle nut leaves]. Procure them somehow and bring them." There ended the dream, or vision. Hemard Panth awoke and looked around;

there was no Swami, and no silver coins. It was his habit to immediately write any dream he had about Baba or any other saint. Because therein was a message or a *leela* that would manifest itself at sometime.

Every year they celebrated the Ganapathi utsav for five days [That is they have Sthapana of Ganapathi for five days and then they do *visarjan* (immersion of the idol). And the visarjan was performed two days ago so he was sure that there would be some *paan* in the house. He asked his wife about it. She replied that there was one bundle left, and it contained about a hundred leaves. Satisfied, he thought about the dream again. It was impossible for him to go to far away Damboli and deliver the paan. So decided to send it to Shirdi. But who would take it to Shirdi? This thought was foremost in his mind. At that very moment he heard some footsteps. Anna Chinchnikar had just reached the landing of the staircase. Hemard Panth was filled with joy. He welcomed him and Anna came into his home, and gave him a packet of *udi.* Anna had just returned from Shirdi and was staying with a friend of his at Bandra. Hemard told Anna about his dream vision and asked him if he knew of anyone going to Shirdi in a day or two. Anna informed him that Bala Sahib Dev was scheduled to leave that Tuesday. Hemard Panth at once brought the paan vida [Bundle of hundred leaves], two supari [beetlenuts], eight anna coin to be offered to Baba and gave them to Anna. That day was Sunday when all this took place.

The next day Anna took the packet and went to Dev's home in Thane. He narrated the dream and Hemard's resolve to offer the paan vida to Baba. Dev gladly accepted the packet and said he would offer it to Baba. The day Dev was to leave for Shirdi, his daughter was unwell. Thus he had to postpone his departure by two days. All this while the paan was with him and there was no way of preventing them from wilting and drying.

On reaching Shirdi he went directly to the Dwarkamai and offered the paan vida. He narrated everything that

140

happened from the beginning to his arrival in Shirdi. Baba received the offering. He put the eight anna coin in His pocket, and kept the supari and paan vida on His *gaadi*. Many devotees' offered Baba fruits, sweets and paan vidas, which Baba accepted but distributed it right away. This paan vida was offered with utmost love and devotion, so He kept it on His gaadi and said, "Aasu dhe sukhlele paane, Maaza vida aahe to rahude" [Roughly Translated – "Let it be, these dried paan leaves, the vida is Mine let them remain here."]

Dev intended to write to Hemard and tell all that transpired at Shirdi. But on the 27th September, Anna and Shama stopped at Thana on their way to Chinchni. They sent a message to Hemard to meet them. He met them and they related in detail all that took place at Shirdi. That very evening he went to Bhau Sahib Dixit's home at Vile Parle to attend the *Gaj Gowri* puja. As it was too late to go home he stayed overnight. In the morning after breakfast he was about to leave when Dixit asked him to listen to the portion being read. Dixit daily read a chapter of the *Eknath Bhagvat*. That day he read the *shloka* that states that when anything is offered with love and devotion, even if it's stale and dry, it is accepted and relished.

Baba took Mahasamadhi on 15th October 1918 exactly a month after this. This wonderful leela was the proof of Baba's love for His devotees. For Hemard Panth it was a positive proof that the wilted dried paan, an offering of devotion was accepted by his Sadguru.

[Ref: *Sai Leela,* Ank 9-10, Year 5, 1926]

Leela 58: Ram Krishna Nana Vagal and Harish Chandra Pithale

Harish Chandra Pithale (photo 31) was a dear friend of Ram Krishna N.Vagal. He worked as a salesman in the Ghram Company. His eldest son who was studying in college, died after a short illness on 11th April, 1910 leaving his wife and a small son behind. The family was grief stricken and did not know where to turn to find solace. At that time Raghunath Sathe Tendulkar was also employed in the same office. On his own he arranged for a *kirtan* to be held on the 6th June at their residence in Santa Cruz. None other than Das Ganu performed the kirtan. The result was that the whole family became totally devoted to Baba. So eager were they to have Baba's darshan that they kept singing 'Darshan De Sai Baba' from morning to night [Das Ganu's *Bhajan*].

On the 23rd April Raghunath informed Vagal that he should apply for a five day leave period a week from that day, as they would be going to Shirdi. But the very next day, his mind kept turning to Baba and he was determined to take a decision. So he placed some chits in front of Baba [That was what Dixit did when he was in doubt]. The chits read 'Do not apply for leave', 'Request Eight days of leave' and the last chit was 'apply for leave today'. The chit that was picked was to apply for 'leave today' itself. He was very surprised as that day he did not feel like applying for leave.

He was astonished when Nandram, Mr Ghram's secretary came to him on his own accord and asked him when he was going on leave. The reason being that Mr Ghram was leaving for Karachi the next day and would not return for a fortnight.

So Pithale had better apply for leave that day itself. He did as advised and had no problem in getting it sanctioned.

That evening he went along with Raghunath Sathe to meet Dabolkar and Dixit. He also got a letter of introduction from Rao Sahib Sathe. That evening Vagal went to Pithale's home and he learned all this from his son who asked him to wait for his father. At 10 p.m. Harish Chandra returned home and informed him that he was to accompany him to Shirdi. Vagal told him that this was impossible, as the department of 'The Examiner Marine Accounts' had opened a branch in Calcutta and seven officers from there were coming on the second of July to take charge of the office in Mumbai. And he had to supervise the transition, which was only a week away. So it was imperative that he be here. Then Harish Chandra said, "Sai Baba has asked you to accompany me. So you apply for leave and you are sure to get it. Just as I got my leave, which is a leela in itself."

Surprised at what he heard Vagal said, "Neither of us have met Baba, then how does He know my name? And when and where did He say this? You like me hence you say this." Harish Chandra said, "When I was returning from Bandra by train I snoozed off for a short while. This happened while the train was on the Bandra bridge and I got a dream. I distinctly heard a voice that said, "bring Ram Krishna with you." "That day was Saturday the 27th June and they were to go to Shirdi on the second of July. Vagal did not have the courage to ask for leave. Daily Harish Chandra would ask him if he had applied for leave.

On that Friday the Head clerk was talking to him when he broached the subject. He asked for leave and was granted leave for four days. That was the day he had to go to the Marine office. There the officer received a telegram from the Calcutta office regarding some work. That work was with him so the officer asked him to postpone his leave by a week.

Vagal then asked him for a day's leave that was for Monday, promising him that he would be back on Tuesday. They left that night and reached Kopergaon at 8 a.m. the next day. The Godavari had overflowed its banks due to heavy rainfall, and the village was water logged. This meant that they would have to take a long circuitous route. That day they happened to meet Mamlatdar Rao Sahib Shakaram Mirikar who told them that he had received a letter from Nagar that the Assistant Collector Mr Madan wanted to visit Shirdi. So they would have to wait for him. Hence they went to Mirkar's home.

Vagal seized the opportunity and asked him about Baba. He said he did visit Baba once, but he did not have too much faith. However, he said that once you meet Baba the desire to visit Shirdi often is irresistible. Vagal also noted that there was a huge photograph of Baba in his living room, which was worshipped with *chandan* and flowers. Madan arrived at about twelve noon, and they set out immediately as Madan had to return the same day.

The group consisted of about twelve people. They reached Shirdi at 4 p.m. Vagal though happy was apprehensive because he had heard that no one could leave Shirdi unless Baba gave permission and he was running out of time. They reached Dwarkamai and Baba was sitting in His usual place near the Katrada with His left hand resting on it. They prostrated before Baba and sat down, close to Baba. Madan sat right in front, behind him Vagal with his family, behind him and last of all Harish Chandra and his family. They happened to be sitting next to the Dhuni.

Shama who was sitting in front of them near the Katra said, "Baba the collector Sahib has come for Darshan." Baba replied, "All right". Baba turned to Madan and gave him His chillum saying, "You have to return today itself? And you should do so as your responsibility is towards the Government".

Vagal wanted to ask Baba about his departure when Harish Chandra fell at Baba's feet. Baba said, "I know your family, your mother had brought you for My darshan [This was a pilgrimage to Akkalkot to have darshan of Swami Samarth; his mother had taken Harish Chandra with her]". Today you don't have to cook. Have prasad at Sathe Wada and from tomorrow you can cook your own meals." Vagal had but a day's leave left, and he was anxious about it with this thought in his mind he prostrated before Baba. The kind Baba stroked his back and said, "Why are you anxious? Be calm and wait." His family could not understand what Baba meant but Vagal was overwhelmed by love and devotion and tears of joy ran down his cheeks. Very humbly he said, "Baba I too work for the Government, and I am running out of leave." Baba replied "Don't worry at all. Now all of you go to the Wada and partake of the prasad." [Ref: *Sai Leela,* Ank 7-10, Year 4, 1926]

Vagal's Return to Work

On Monday morning they had darshan. His nephew, performed ritualistic puja, and sang aarti of Narayan Maharaj. Baba listened to the aarti with great joy. Then He asked them to go to the wada, as it would rain. Indeed a little while later it did rain. The downpour continued for three days. It was a delay of another two days for Vagal. On Wednesday Baba said, they could leave for Mumbai. After taking udi, prasad and Baba's blessings they left and reached Kopergaon in the evening. There they met Mamaltdar Yashwant Rao who happened to be near the Godavari. He invited them to his home and looked after them very well. He also asked them to stay with him for the night. As they did want to impose on him, he made arrangements for their stay in a bungalow nearby. The next day after a bath in the Godavari they had darshan of the Dutta Mandir and caught the 9 a.m. train. The connecting Mail from Manmad was on time and they had a comfortable journey to Mumbai. The next day he went to work. To his surprise his superior was not upset with his delay in joining work. However he asked him as to what had happened. Vagal told him all that had transpired, to that he said, "All right". The leave was granted and the project was sent to Calcutta fifteen days later.

Leela 59:   **Harish Chandra and his Epileptic Son**

This leela is described in the *Shri Sai Satcharita*, Chapter 26. Here some more details are given. As it was stated earlier Harish Chandra and his family sat near the Dhuni. As they got up to go to the wada, his third son Dwarakanath (photo 32), also did the same. This child had been suffering from a convulsive disorder probably epilepsy for a long time. He got an attack right there, and nearly fell into the Dhuni. His mother noticed the attack was about to take place and with great presence of mind held the child.

The mother was frightened and distraught, and she wept inconsolably. Baba said, "Aaye don't be frightened. Allah Malik will make him all right" and taking *udi* from the Dhuni applied it on his forehead. Dwaraka Nath recovered and thenceforth never had a convulsion again. He grew up to be a fine gentleman. Got married and had two sons. After his father's death his younger brother Chandra Kanth managed his father's business, according to his mother's wishes

[Ref: Sai Leela, Ank 7-10, Year 4, 1926]

Leela 60: Purushotham R.Avasthi and Radha Krishna Mayi's Leelas

Avasthi came to Shirdi in 1914 with M.B. Rege. Since Baba had advised Rege to stay with Aayi, he did so every time he visited Shirdi. When they both came to Shirdi they naturally stayed with Aayi. And Avasthi became very close to her. In early November 1917 Aayi took samadhi [died]. Though she had passed away she gave Avasthi some wonderful experiences. The night of her demise Avasthi was mentally thanking her for the spiritual guidance she had given him. Aayi then enabled him to have her darshan.

The next morning while he was in a light slumber he heard Abdul Bhai calling him. He ran to open the door, and looked around. There was no Abdul Bhai, but a neighbour was picking some flowers to offer to Baba. It was so real that he asked the man whether some man had come there. On the third day he received a letter from Vaman Rao Patel stating that Aayi had passed away.

In May of 1918 he went to Shirdi with his younger sister, and sister-in-law. They stayed in Aayi's house. That evening they wanted to offer '*pitla bhakar*' as *naivedya*. The two ladies tried to light the *chule* [hearth] but no matter what they did, it would just not light. They were thinking about Aayi and how she happily made prasad for Baba. When to their astonishment they saw Aayi coming down the steps from the floor above. Not only did she sat down but blew into the *chule* fire and ignited it also. Then the ladies made delicious '*pitla bhakar*' and offered it to Baba. Aayi thus gave them *sakshatkar*. It was so real that Avasthe and his family felt that Aayi was alive and with them right there. After some time, when they realised that Aayi had passed away, they were full of wonder.

[Ref: *Sai Leela*, Punyathithi Ank, July August, September,1952]

Leela 61:   **Avasthi's Prasad**

Once the ladies in his family, along with their friends gathered together and performed *bhajans* and *satsang* in the puja room. This went on for a long time and it was very late at night. Then suddenly there was the aroma of roses, which became so overpowering that the ladies stopped the bhajans and went to their rooms.

On the third day Avasthi had an irresistible desire to offer prasad to Baba. He told his family about it. Two of his sister-in-laws, took a quantity of rice to make the prasad and washed it. Both were unaware that the other had washed the rice. Then both of them entered the kitchen carrying the washed rice. Now what was to be done with so much rice. Avasthi at once said that they could prepare kesar bhath [Sweet rice prepared with saffron] as Baba was very fond of it. Then Avasthi offered it to Baba with love and devotion. No sooner had this been done, he received a letter that Baba had taken Mahasamadhi. A short while later, a dear friend of his visited him. And hearing about Baba's *niryan* was very surprised. He told Avasthi that in the Muslim faith it was a ritual and custom to offer meetha chawal [kesar bath] on the third day after death.

Leela 62:   **Madhav Rao Deshpande**
[Shama]

It is impossible to write or try to figure out the relationship between Baba and Shama. The *rinanubandh* between these two was deep, and unfathomable. It is apt to say that the relationship can be compared to that of Lord Krishna and Arjuna. In fact, many comparisons are evident. Many of the conversations they had are given in the leelas below.

Shama as Baba called him was born to a Yajurvedi Dehsasth Brahmin family who resided in Nimon Gaon. His family came to Shirdi when he was two-years-old and made Shirdi their home. He studied in Shirdi and later became a school teacher. The school was next to the Dwarkamai. That was later turned into a stable for Shyam Karan [Baba's Horse]. Baba called Madhav Rao 'Shama' or more often 'Shamyaa', the very tone of it was full of love and caring. The word 'Shyam' in Sanskrit means black, but a flawless, and pleasing black colour. 'Shama' is also used to mean holy or pure, as in the holy Tulsi, or the holy Yamuna River. Used as a prefix in 'Shyam-Sunder' to mean Shri Krishna. Or as in 'Shyam-Kant' the name of Lord Shiva. Or in 'Shyam-Karn' the Ashwamedha horse, that was holy and undefeatable.

The relation between Baba and Shama was mind-boggling. One can best describe it as *shakha* [a dear friend]. It was the kind of relation that Arjun had with Lord Krishna. The love that Baba had for Shama is mentioned in various chapters of the *Shri Sai Satcharita* as in Chapter 35. Mrs Aurangabadakar asked Shama to help her in opening her heart to Baba, as she was seeking a cure for her infertility. Shama waited for the right opportunity. One day Baba was in a joyful mood and he pinched Shama's cheek. Shama pretended to be offended. When Baba said, "In the seventy-two generations that we have been together have I ever touched you? Just try and remember." The *rinanubandh* spanned a period of seventy-two generations.

Once Kaka Sahib came to the Dwarkamai and prostrated at Baba's feet. Baba asked him what he wanted. Kaka with tears in his eyes said, " I want You to be with me always." To that Baba replied, "Keep Shamya with you and know that I am with you." After that Kaka kept Shama with him. In *Shri Sai Satcharita* Chapter 22, Bala Sahib Mirikar visited Shirdi and after darshan he wanted to return to Chitale.

Baba knowing that he was to have an encounter with a snake averts it by asking him to take Shama with him. For it was as good as Baba going with him. Shama on the other hand called Baba 'Deva' but often took liberties with Him. The other devotees did not have the courage to ask Baba to come and sit for lunch. Shama however, after the aarti was over would say "Deva get up and go and take Your seat. And make Kaala of the prasad." Baba without saying one word would get up and sit near the Nimbar.

Leela 63:   Shama's Quest to Know the Ramayana

Once Shama (photo 60) asked Baba " Kaya Re" slang usually used amongst friends]. Deva it is written in the Ramayan that Lord Rama got a bridge built by one crore of monkeys. This bridge spanned the sea, so Rama could cross it and reach Lanka. There he waged war with Ravana and vanquished him. Deva is this true?" Baba said, "Yes, this is

true. The sea is real Shama and Lord Rama was really there."
Shama then said, "Deva, where did so many monkeys sit? And
how did they sit?" Baba replied, "They sat on the trees and
clung to the branches. They looked like myriads of ants."
Shama then said, "Did You see this with your own eyes?' Baba
said, "Yes, Yes I saw this with My Own eyes. All right Shama."
Shama then said, "When I first saw You here You hardly had
a stubble of moustache. Then how and when did You go to
see the 'Vanar Sena Re." Baba said, "Shamyaa you and I have
been together for many generations. I remember them but
you do not." In wonder Shama said, "How old were you then?"
Baba.

Baba said, "Just as you see Me now." Shama could not
grasp the fact that Baba was, is and will be the same forever.
Then he said, "Is this really true?" Baba said, "Have I ever lied
sitting here in the Dwarkamai? What I say is true. I swear by
you." Once Shri Krishna said the same thing to Arjun. In the
Dnyaneshwari shlok 1368, Krishna says, "Do not entertain any
misgivings about what I say. I swear by you to guarantee its
truth."

Leela 64: **Shama Had an Eye Infection**

The devotees came to Baba for relief from their physical
ailments, and Baba would cure them. It was a common
sight to see Baba sitting in the Dwarkamai and giving udi the
panacea for all the troubles of life. Once Shama had a
fulminating eye infection. His eyes were red, swollen and
watered profusely. He tried various ointments, and pills. But
the infection went from bad to worse. The swelling increased
and the pain became quite unbearable. At last he went to
Baba and confronted Him. Baba asked him if all was well.

This upset him even more and he said, angrily, "Deva I haven't seen such a callous, uncaring, and unconcerned God like You. You cure the whole of humanity. For the past four days I am in agony, my eyes are swollen, watering incessantly, and the pain is unbearable. Because of the throbbing I am crying, shouting and dying of pain, but You are oblivious of this. Aren't You ashamed of Yourself? Are You blind? Are You deaf too? What use is such a God? If by tomorrow my eyes are not cured, I will drive You out of the Dwarkamai or my name is not Shama"

Baba said, "Ugach, vat vat karu nakos Shamyaa, saath meeryach daane ugaal aani de doolyath ghalun mange bhag thuje doole vingaavani hothil" [Shamyaa, don't grumble for nothing. Take seven black pepper seeds and boil them in some water and put this in your eyes. And your eyes will become crystal clear. Here take this Udi and go.]" This infuriated Shama further, and he said, "Deva You think You are very smart? Where on earth did You learn this Vaidgiri? I will put the pepper in my eyes and my eyes will burst. How great is Your prescription? It's a prescription only to burst people's eyes." Baba calmly said, "Don't act smart Shamyaa. Go and do what I said, and if your eyes don't become clear then you can get angry." Although Madhav Rao said all this to Baba; he had utmost faith in Baba's words. Shama then did as he was told and Lo! his eyes became crystal clear instantaneously. Arjun once said the same to Shri Krishna [*Dnyaneshwari*, Chapter 3, verse 8] – "If a physician after examining a patient puts poison in the medicine, and administers it to the patient. Are there any chances of the patient's survival?"

[Ref: *Shirdi Che Sai Baba,* written by Dr Keshev B.Gavankar]

Leela 65:   **Baba Shows Shama
the Trilok (Three Worlds)**

Once Shama asked Baba whether there really was a
'Trilok'. In his characteristic way he said, " Deva, is there
a Brahma Lok, Vishnu Lok, and Shiv Lok Re?" Baba replied in
the affirmative. Shama immediately said, "Arre Deva why don't
You show it to me?" Baba explained to him that all the wealth
and opulence that the Gods had though it was full of grandeur
was very small for them. And that, this kind of wealth was not
for them. He said, "Yahek ishwarya pramane hey Devache
Aishwarya hey tooch aah hey." Shama however insisted on
seeing it. Then Baba asked him to close his eyes and then
open them. And Lo! Shama could see Brahma Lok. He saw
the most beautiful, ornate diamond studded throne on which
Brahma was sitting. He was holding court with his ministrels.
They too were sitting on beautiful, golden chairs studded with
gems. There was so much of gold and gems that it was
indescribable. Baba said, "Shama this is Satya Lok, and this is
Brahma Dev." Baba then asked him to open and close his
eyes again and He showed him Vaikunth Lok. Lastly He showed
him Kailash Lok. Each time he saw one of the Loks, Baba
explained to him what he was seeing and who the presiding
deity was. Shama was overwhelmed by what he saw. He was
slightly frightened and at the same time joyful to see the
abundance of wealth and oppulence. Again Baba emphasised,
"Shama all this is not for us, our goal is quite unusual." Shama
could see all this because Baba gave him *divia drishti* [cosmic
vision]. This is a word I have coined, as there is no word in

the English language that can be used. It conveys the meaning that 'Evolved souls can visualise the abode of the Gods.'

Shri Krishna also gave Arjuna 'divia drishti' so he could see him as God and not as his friend.

[Ref: *Shirdi Che Sai Baba*, written by Dr Keshev B.Gavankar]

Leela 66:   Shama and the Vishnu Shashranaam

Just as Lord Krishna bestowed his grace upon Arjuna and Uddhav, so did Baba bestow His Grace on Shama. But the method was very different. Baba's method was unusual, and unfathomable.

Once a Ram Dasi came to Shirdi, he took his *aasan* in the Sabha Mandap of the Dwarkamai. Every morning he would read the pothi. One day Baba had a stomachache. Shama who was nearby, asked Him what the matter was. Baba said, "I have a terrible stomachache," Then He asked the Ram Dasi to go and fetch some *Sonamukhi* as it would relieve Him of His pain. As soon as the Ram Dasi left, Baba left His seat and went and took the *Vishnu Sahasranam* from the bundle of books, belonging to the Ram Dasi. Baba then gave it to Shama and asked him to keep it. Shama was upset and said, "I don't want Your Pothi." Baba however insisted that he keep it. Shama angrily said, "Deva first You lied saying You had a stomachache, then You went and stole his book. You steal the book and give it to someone, and that person is thought to be a robber. You on the other hand talk sweetly to the onlookers, so that Your name remains unblemished. From where did You learn to lie and steal *re*?" To that Baba replied, "Arre Shama, is this lying and stealing"? Just as Shri Krishna talked sweetly to the

154

gopis and then stole their butter, and then lied that he had not done so. At this moment Shama was very angry and he said, "You are a great God! You lie, and steal, but does anyone call You a liar, or a robber? I must be mad because I listen to You, and do as You say. I tolerate whatever You do and say. To top it all You talk sweetly, swear by my feet and neck and use devious, and cunning ways to get Your work done. You say one thing and do another."

The Ram Dasi returned from the market at that very moment. And seeing the *Vishnu Shashranaam* in Shama's hand got extremely angry. He called Shama a thief and a schemer. Baba pacified him and said, "Arre! Ram Dasyia, You profess to be a Ram Dasi, wear orche and do Bhakti yet you can't control your anger. You are so possessive of a book. Aren't you ashamed to wear orche, and not honour it or know its significance? Shama don't get upset at his outburst take this *Udi* and go." This leela is described in *Shri Sai Satcharita*, Chapter 27. A few more details are given here. Shama came to Shirdi from Nimon Gaon when he was two-years-old. He studied up to seventh class in Marathi medium. As he lived in this remote village, he was not exposed to people who spoke correct or good Marathi. His way of speaking was like a rustic. Though he could read Marathi well, he knew no Sanskrit. Baba in His mercy gave him the *Vishnu Shasranaam* and asked him to recite it. This was an impossible task, but for Baba's Grace, he not only learned it by heart. He could recite it correctly, and explain its meaning. A time came when scholars like Kaka Dixit and Professor Narke came to him for explanation of the complicated Sanskrit phrases.

[Ref: *Shirdi Che Sai Baba* written by Dr Keshev B.Gavankar]

Leela 67: **Shama and Money**

Shama did a few jobs before he devoted his life to Baba. He worked as an assistant master in the Junior School that was adjacent to the Dwarkamai. Then he took up the post of 'Patil' of Astha Gaon, a village about twenty miles from Shirdi.

Simultaneously he learned Ayurveda and administered '*jadi buty*' [plants with medicinal value] to the sick and ailing. At that time he was close to Baba and their *rinanubandhic* relation was established. Shama was famous for his Ayurvedic skill and many famous people from Mumbai came to consult him. Interestingly, he did not go to any school to learn Ayurveda. He read various books and was self-taught. Being astute he watched Baba give the devotees herbs and poultices, and learned how to administer them. Armed with this knowledge, he treated cases that other doctors had given up. They came to him from far and wide. Whenever he gave or administered medicines, he never failed to mix a little *udi* in the medicines. And only after taking Baba's name would he start the treatment. How then could he fail?

The house in Shirdi belonged to Shama and that was where he lived till Baba's Mahasamadhi. In Nimon Gaon the Deshpande's were vatandars [tax collectors] and had vast acres of land. They also received some income from that post. Nasik, Sinner and Kopergaon paid some amount of money collected from taxes. Shama however lost his income because he stayed at Baba's side all the time and had no time to practise Ayurveda.

Baba distributed vast amounts of money on a daily basis [about four to five hundred rupees a day]. He would give Tatya, Ramachandra and Bayaji Patil money every day. Some devotees received an income from Baba. Shama however did not receive any money from Baba. One day Shama said, "Deva people say You are compassionate and caring. As You give the devotees whatever they want. To some You give a husband or wife, to others children, And yet to others You give money or wealth. While I am at Your feet all the time. Yet You give me not a pie. I can't even get money from You to buy some tobacco How does this happen? I don't think there is anyone as stingy as You in this world Deva. You tie a rag around Your head, sit in this *masjid* and smoke a *chillum*, and then go around this village begging for food and eat it. Then how can You give me anything? Now everyone calls You God, but who made You God, but me? Otherwise everyone would be calling You a begging Fakir." Baba was calm during this outburst, then He said, "Shama money is not for you, your mission is quite unusual."

On the other hand, Baba sent many of his 'orthodox' devotees to have their meals with Shama. So Shama was rather poor in the worldly sense, but Baba gave him spiritual gifts that were invaluable. Baba often gave him religious books, Pothis and Shama read and reread, them with great zeal. Thus he collected spiritual wealth. Before Baba's Mahasamadhi he had quite a collection of books. He was able to explain and expound the intricate verses therein at ease.

The other spiritual gift that Baba gave was to send Shama on pilgrimages. In fact, Shama had visited all the 'Holy Sites' across the length and breadth of India. Kashi, Char Dham and Jaganath Puri were some of the holy sites he visited.

Every day Baba received numerous letters and Shama would read them aloud to Baba. And according to Baba's orders reply to them. If any *bhakta* had sent any money he would go and collect the money from the post office and hand it over to Baba. This he did diligently and never failed to give the exact amount to Baba. Once a bhakta had sent a money order for two rupees, Shama went and collected it from the post office.

On his way back, he changed his intention of returning it to the Baba. He hid the money in the Dwarkamai. There was a huge door for the room that housed the *rath*. He kept the money over that door in a crevice near the wall. The Omnipresent Baba said not a word. Shama however thought, "How will Deva know this"?

Then disaster struck. One night there was a theft in his home, and the thief robbed him of two hundred and fifty rupees. He searched for it everywhere, reported it to the police, but it was futile. There was no trace of the thief or his money. Then in desperation he went to Baba and said, "Baba there was a theft in my home, and the thief stole two hundred and fifty rupees. Do You feel good about this? That a poor man like me lost so much of money. Arre Deva who can I tell my tale of woe to but You?" Baba calmly heard what he had to say and said, "Arre Shamyaa what is the matter? Because there was a theft, and you lost money, you come to Me with your complaint. But when My two rupees were stolen to whom should I complain?" Shama understood the meaning of Baba's words. But continued " Arre Deva so You, caused this robbery to happen. You are great because Your two rupees were stolen You caused two hundred and fifty rupees to be stolen from a poor man like me. What kind of punishment is this? I lost two hundred and fifty rupees, while You lost only two rupees. What kind of justice is this?" Baba said, "The value of two hundred and fifty rupees for a poor man like you, has the same value of two rupees for a Fakir like Me."

[Ref: *Sai Leela*, Ank 5, year 17, 1940]

Leela 68:   **Shama Visits Nagpur**

Shama was serene by nature and mature in his way of dealings. Though he spoke to Baba like a friend he had the utmost regard for Him. Once he visited Nagpur and Amravati and returned to Shirdi in the afternoon. On his return he came straight to the Dwarkamai. Baba asked him, "Arre Shamyaa what were the places that you visited." Shama told Him that he had visited Nagpur. Baba said, "Arre Shama did you go to South Nagpur? There is a golden tree there did you see it?" Immediately Shama replied, "Yes Baba when I was at Nagpur I did visit south Nagpur, Bhosle's [Raojee Raja's] garden and had darshan of Shri Tajuddin Baba." Instinctively Shama knew that Baba was referring to Tajuddin Sahib (photo 7) as the golden tree. Then Baba asked him what where the other places he visited. Eagerly Shama said, that he went to Amravati after that. There he had the darshan of Shri Narayan Maharaj in the tiny village of Bet in Ked Gaon. Then he told Baba that Narayan Maharaj had a 'big' durbar, and thousands of people went for his darshan. This he repeated again and again. Ganesh Govind Narke who was seated there was rather apprehensive, and was eager to hear Baba's reply. Baba was silent for sometime then He said, " It's like this Shama, only your father is your father. No matter how much he may beat you, shout at you, disagree with you, or punish you. He will always have sympathy and empathy for you, as no one else will. I am your father, so what have you to do with others?"

In His characteristic way Baba taught Shama a valuable lesson. And that was as follows – "Do not look down or talk ill of others, especially a Satpurush for the ill effects of it will be seen on the future generations. Your Guru and Father should

159

be treated with love and respect, do whatever Seva you can for both of them. Have total faith in them." Narke added "Baba sent me and my family to various 'Holy Places' that were charged with spiritual energy. He also encouraged His devotees to continue praying to their 'ishtadevta' with full faith"

[Ref: *Sai Leela*, Ank 5, Year 17, 1940]

Leela 69:   Shama and Ekadashi Fast

Once a bhakta came to meet Baba and offered Him hot roasted *jawari*. Baba said, "Here Shama this is for you" Shama being very orthodox said angrily, "Deva don't You have any shame. Today is the big *ekadashi*, and You are asking me to eat jawari, thus I will incur a sin. Go I won't take it." Baba pacified him saying, "All right Shamyaa don't take it."

In the *Dnyaneshwari*, Chapter three Arjun says to Lord Krishna something on the same lines. On another occasion a devotee asked Baba whether one should or should not eat onions on *ekadashi*. Baba replied that one should not. The devotee persisted saying, "If onions are *Kand*, [tuber Family] then why can't one eat them."? Baba said, "Then eat them" Shama at once said, " Arre Deva why do You talk thus? First You say don't eat onions then You say eat them. We are ignorant hence we ask You." Baba said "Sitting in the Dwarkamai I never speak lies. I swear by your feet Shamyaa. On ekadashi one should not eat onions. But if one has to eat it, because of its effect on the body one should have the capability to digest it. Now take this udi and go."

[Ref: *Shirdi Che Sai Baba* written by Dr Keshev Gavankar]

Shama did not perform the ritualistic puja to Baba, like many other devotees. But had intense faith in Baba. This faith is impossible to describe. In Marathi it is said to be "Baba che allot annaya, ekanista, nirsim bhakti" [Roughly Translated – utter devotion, one pointed, concentrated, and selfless bhakti] Shama with each and every breath of his was performing *jaap* or *naam smaran*. In *Shirdi Diary* the entry for eighth December 1911 is as follows – "Madhavrao Deshpande was here and fell asleep. I saw with my own eyes and heard with my own ears what I only read about but never experienced. With every outgoing and indrawing breath, comes the clear sound of 'Sayin Nath Maharaj, Sayin Nath Baba'. This sound is clear as can be and when Madhavrao snores, the words can be heard at a distance. This is really wonderful." Baba would give Shama udi every time he came or went from the Dwarkamai and that was often. Shama would take it home and collect it in a huge heap. With great devotion and care, he placed it in a corner of his home. His wife was unaware of this. After Baba took Mahasamadhi he would take some udi and give it to the needy with wonderful results. Once Shama had gone to Mumbai. His wife while cleaning the house saw the heap of udi and she took it out to throw away. There at Mumbai, Shama had a vision of Baba who said, "Shamyaa, the Udi I gave you with My own hands, and you carefully preserved is going to be thrown out. Go quickly and keep it safely." Shama went to Shirdi as quickly as he could. There he realised that what Baba said was true. A whole book can be written on Shama.

Shama's Family

In brief I will write about his family. Shama was born in Shake 1782 Margashish Shu I I Panchimi [The year 1880]. His mother was his father's fourth wife. The first three could not bear any children, so his father married Lakshman Mama Kulkarni's sister. Shama was the eldest son. He had two younger brothers – Kashinath Balwant who was adopted by the family and was named Ganesh Shredhar, and Bappajee Balwant *(Shri Sai Satcharita*, Chapter 34). Shama was married twice. His first wife was Savitri Bai, daughter of Gopal Katchwar Kulkarni of Nimon; she had a son named Eknath. His second wife was Dwarka Bai she had two sons – Udavrao and Jaganath Panth and a daughter named Baby Tai.

When the Shirdi Sai Baba Sansthan was formed Shama was staying in Dixit wada. About four months before he took Samadhi [expired] there was some misunderstanding and Shama was asked to vacate Dixit wada within two months. He did so and came back to his home which is near Baba's Dwarkamai. Shama was a healthy villager, eighty-years-old. On Wednesday at about twelve noon he lost consciousness. And the next day Thursday, 16th April, 1944 at night he breathed his last and became one with his Sadguru.

[Ref: *Sai Leela*, Ank 1, Year 33, 1956]

Leela 70:   **Ramachandra M Adkar**

Ramachandra was born to Madhav Rao Vaman and Ganga Bai Adkar on 14th March, 1915. Madhav Rao was an ascetic by nature and often went on pilgrimage to Pandharpur. Once Madhav Rao went to Shirdi and was serving Baba. One day when he was in Dwarkamai with Baba, Baba said, "Madhav Rao two men will come to take you home, you better go. You will beget a son, and you should name him Ram." A short while later his father-in-law and father came to Dwarkamai. Both pleaded with Baba saying, "Baba, do send this Madhav Rao home. Though married he shirks his responsibilities." Baba replied, "He will accompany you." Thus Madhav Rao went home and a year later a son was born. He was named Ramachandra. Ganga Bai brought the young child for Baba's darshan and blessings. His mother died two years later and his maternal grandparents brought up Ram.

Ramachandra (photo 53) studied up to 5th Class in Marathi medium. His father was a linguist and taught him to read and write Urdu. When he grew up he sought the job of a schoolmaster, but was appointed as a head master. Thus he was in charge of four schools. Three months later he was married to Mathura Bai Kulkarni. They stayed in their father's home in Barsi, where he continued to work as headmaster. They had two sons and three daughters. He retired in 1972 and in 1980 moved to Pune where he is currently staying.

With Baba's blessings and grace his children are leading fruitful and comfortable lives.

Leela 71: Gopal Rao Somnath Nimonkar

He was born on *Makar Sankrant* in Nimon (Sangamner district) to Somnath and Deshpande. He was well educated, studied in SP College, Pune and did BA. LLB. He had mastered Sanskrit, English and Astrology. His father who was a famous astrologer influenced his love for astrology. Besides, he excelled in Yoga, and was highly spiritually evolved.

When his parents took him to Baba as a child, Baba held him in His lap. And covering him with a shawl said, "call him Eknath". Somnath (photo 51) was rather uncomfortable as he had already christened him Gopal Rao. Baba then said, "He is my Eknath." He is the little boy standing next to Nana Sahib in the Lendi Baugh procession. In the photograph taken in 1916. [As vouched by his daughter].

He prospered and was famous in Ahmednagar for his oratory and law practice. Many students learned about 'fighting cases' from him. He had a flare for the English language.

Sanskrit however was his love. He would recite the *Vishnu Sahasranam* and *Rudra Abhisek*, and various *suktas* in a deep resonant voice, filling his home with sanctified vibrations. For 22 years he and his fellow lawyers did *padyatra*, from Eknath's Paithan to Matherdev [Pathardi district] on Mahashivratri. There he performed Rudra Abhisek. Was it any wonder that Baba called him" My Eknath."

He survived his first heart attack at the age of 73. Then at age of 84 he took Samadhi on 19th December 1997. He will always be remembered by us and all Baba devotees for being instrumental in continuing the sacred tradition of taking the flag from Pune to Shirdi on Ram Navami day (*Shri Sai Satcharitra*, Chapter 6, the 'Ram Navami' celebrations in Shirdi are described). Every year two flags were taken out in procession and then tied to the spire of the Dwarkamai. One of these came from Nimonkar's home, and the other came from Dammu Anna's home. It was this tradition that Gopal Rao kept alive.

Leela 72: **Sarojini Muley**
[Kaka Sahib Mahajini's Daughter]

Both her parents were devoted to Baba. Hence, she was inculcated into the Bhakti Marg very early in life. Sarojini was born on 2nd May 1910 at Bandra. She was the daughter of Lakshman Ganesh Mahajini, whom Baba called 'Kaka.' Mention is made of him in various places in the *Shri Sai Satcharita* Chapter12, Chapter 35. Sarojini first visited Shirdi in 1918 along with her father. Baba on seeing her beckoned her to come close and said, "She is My Maina [sparrow], Then he sat her on His lap. She visited Shirdi often with her father. Baba asked them to stay at Shama's home. The stay would often be for five to seven days even sometime longer, depending on when Baba gave them permission to leave.

Sarojini (photo 66) did her primary education at the Hujurpaga High School, Pune. She learned classical music. She played the harmonium and dilruba, as she was very talented and mastered both instruments. Having successfully passed many examinations, she had numerous certificates. She married Bhaskar Vinayak Muley in 1928 and moved to Indore. Her husband worked in the Holkar State Offices at first. And later was in the administrative services of Madhya Pradesh. On retiring from the services he did a lot of social work, along with his wife. Sarojini was an office bearer of the Tukogang Bhagani Mandal and did various charity projects.

Once Kaka visited Shirdi and Baba said, "I had visited your home 'Anand Ashram' in Pune, and found the door locked". On returning home he questioned his wife about it? She confirmed it saying, "she had gone to the Ram Mandir at that time". Sarojini tirelessly worked for Shirdi Sai Baba Sansthan. She was the president of the annual *Sai Leela Magazine* meeting in 1981. She took samadhi on 16th November, 1998. Her daughter with her family live in Indore.

Leela 73: **Baba's Pocket**

Baba's pocket was rather small; it could hold about two hundred to three hundred rupees as coins. Yet Baba took out five hundred to one thousand rupees from His pocket. It was Kuber's treasury. As a rule Baba did not keep money in His hand. Nor did He accept rupee bills, if a devotee wished to give dakshina and it was in the form of bills He asked him to change it or did so Himself. Whatever dakshina He got, He put it in His pocket. He would time and again put His hand in His pocket and take out the exact amount mentioned. Daily He distributed about two hundred to three hundred rupees, and did not stop it till His Mahasamadhi.

He gave Bade Baba fifty-five rupees every day. The villagers got envious, and asked Bade Baba to build a *vess* [gate] with the money. He refused, so they drove him away to Neemgaon. Baba would go to Lendi Baugh to give him money. This bothered the villagers as Baba had to go to Lendi Baugh and wait there for the Bade Baba.

So they called Bade Baba back, but he spent his money indiscriminately. He also had to pay tax on the income. Two months after Baba's Mahasamadhi he was begging for a living. Baba often said, "Ha Saicha paisa hey, Thayacha sadd upyog kaara. Naahi thar tumcha sansar rakh rangoli hoyael" [Roughly Translated – "This is Sai's money use it discriminatively or your life will be reduced to ashes and dust."]. Baba looked at money or *Aishwarya* (wealth) as a hindrance. Though, He felt it was a necessity, and ought to be used wisely.

In those days the coins were made of silver, and no other alloy was mixed with it. Being pure silver it would retain heat. Thus, when the devotee gave dakshina, the heat from his hands, or himself would be transferred to Baba's hands. Hence, Baba would take upon Himself the karmic *Prarabdha* of that person. Baba did not accept money in the form of bills, as paper would burn easily but not silver.

He had a small cloth pouch in which he kept some coins. He tied the pouch tightly so that the coins would not jingle. Then He kept the pouch in His pocket. After the noon meal was over, and the devotees had gone home, Baba would take out the pouch, and take out the coin. Then He would rub each coin, saying, "Hey Kaka Cha, Hey Nana Cha." If anyone entered the Sanctum Sanctorum at that time He hid the pouch. Baba had rubbed the coins so much that the impressions on them had faded. Thus Baba rubbed off their bad karmas.

The bhaktas that were given 'the pocket' by Baba, were stunned by the outcome. Tatya Kote had no children though he had two wives, after receiving the pockets (photo 58 and 59). He had three sons. In the afternoon when all the devotees had gone home Baba would stitch the torn pocket. On the other hand Jyotindra with the money in the pocket (photo 56) was able to buy a home in the Tata building (photo 73).

Tata Building Bandra, Mumbai Where the Tarkhads' Lived

"Kay Karve Aayi aaj gelo mee vandra see jaisa Roje Naahi, Kavaya Piyavaya Paje Upasi Maj Yava Lagele" [*Shri Sai Satcharita*, chapter 9, Ovi 107,109]

"What could I do O Mother? Today like every day I went to Bandra, but there was neither gruel nor food. Nothing was there to eat or drink so I had to return," said Baba.

"Kaisa paha rinanubandhi Kavad Hoithe Jari Bandh. Tari me pravesh lo swachand Kaun prathibandh maj kari" [Look at this rinanubandh although the door was closed, still I entered at my own will who is to prevent me]. The owner was not at home. My intestines were growling with hunger at the height of noon without food. I had to return," said Baba to Mrs.Tarkhad, who along with Jyotindra were seated in Dwarkamai. Jyotindra was reluctant to accompany his mother to Shirdi. He was not sure that his father would offer *naivedya* daily to Baba in the photograph and then have his meals. His father promised him that he would definitely to do so. But one day in haste he went to work and forgot to offer naivedya. Then Baba sitting in the Dwarkamai said the above words. It was this house in Bandra that Baba had visited.

Leela of the Copper Paisa

Baba and Jyotindra Tarkhad had deep *rinanubandhic* ties with each other. Jyotindra was studying in St. Xaviers School; it was his habit to have lunch daily at an Iranian restaurant across the street. One day after having lunch he was crossing the street, when a fakir accosted him and asked for *biksha*.

The kind lad reached into his pocket and gave Him one paisa coin [a copper coin with a hole in the centre and proceeded to school. However, the fakir stopped him and told him that it was a one paisa coin of 1894. Baffled Jyotindra told Him that it was okay as he got a daily allowance of four annas for lunch. He also added that the coin was of the current year so the Fakir ought not worry. The Fakir laughed and said, "Allaha bhalla karega".

As the days rolled by this incident faded from his memory. Mrs Tarkhad was tormented by headaches, and their intensity and frequency also increased. On the advice of Pir Maulana Sahib she decided to go to Shirdi. Taking Jyotindra with her they made the pilgrimage to meet Baba. They went to the Dwarkamai and Baba welcomed them as He was waiting for them. Baba of course cured Mrs Tarkhad of her headaches [This leela of 'the cure' is given elsewhere]. Then turning to Jyotindra Baba said, "Bhau have you recognised Me?" As Jyotindra did not, Baba said, "Try and remember?" Then Baba put His hand in His pocket and took out the copper coin. And showing it to Jyotindra said, "Don't you remember this copper coin dated 1894?. That Fakir you gave alms to was none other than Me."

Then Baba gave him the coin and said, "Keep this coin and preserve it carefully. It will breed a multitude of paisas" Jyotindra took the coin and put it to good use. Daily he used to light a *ghee diya* so he placed the coin at the base and through the hole in the center stood the wick which he would light. What a wonderful way to use the coin!

Leela 74: **Savitri Bai Raghunath Tendulkar**

Savitri Bai (photo 34) lived with her family in Bandra Mumbai. She and her family were devoted to Baba. Every Thursday she made a pilgrimage to Shirdi carrying *prasad* and a garland made of *Bakul* flowers. In the compound of her Bandra home there was a bakul tree. The tree gave an abundance of flowers for three months and then the flowers started waning. Early in the morning the tree would shed myriads of flowers. Savitri Bai would gather these flowers and offer them to Baba. It was a ritual that she liked to do daily. She had a small photograph of Baba and she performed puja to it. First she made a bed of flowers and then placed the photograph on it. Meticulously she made garlands of various sizes and placed them on the photograph. The rest of the flowers she offered doing *naam jap.* Thus mounds of flowers were in front of the photograph.

On one of her visits to Shirdi, Baba was sitting with a large group of people, when He pointed to her and said, "I was not in Shirdi for the last three months. I was in Mayie's home. She smothered Me with bakul flowers. I am intoxicated by their smell" (*Shri Sai Satcharita*, Chapters 2 and 29).

Her son Bapu was very hyperactive when he was young. So Savatri Bai brought him to Shirdi and left him with Baba. On one of her visits she saw that the boy was running a high temperature. He was lying in a corner near the Dhuni Maa groaning and moaning. At once she asked Baba why this was so. Baba calmly replied, "Don't worry Mayi he will be all right, just give him a little *udi* mixed in water." She did as she was told and to her surprise the boy recovered after some time.

Savitri Bai and her family belonged to the Warkari Sampradaya. Though her family was of a religious bent, Savitri Bai was very progressive for her times. She wrote the bhajan mala in the form of "padas, and abhangs." These were about her experiences of Baba's *leelas* and divinity. She was a prolific writer and wrote articles for the *Sai Leela* Magazine.

The small photograph that Baba gave Savitri Bai is with her descendants. It has a lot of sentimental value, so much so that the family will not wipe it, as they do not want to wipe off Baba's touch.

Madhav Rao Tendulkar

Savitri Bai and Raghunath (photo 35) had four children Bapu was the youngest child. Mention is made of him in *Shri Sai Satcharita*, Chapter 29, when Baba assured his mother of success in the MBBS exam. His name was Madhav Rao (photo 36). He was born in 1898. As a child he was rather hyperactive, so his mother brought him to Shirdi and left him with Baba.

At that time he was about eight-years-old. When Baba went for *bhiksha*, he would accompany Him. Bapu would then run ahead and collect the bhiksha. Finally when Baba would return after His bhiksha rounds Bapu was the first to receive Baba's bhiksha prasad. Fortunate was this child, as he was looked after by Baba daily. Madhav Rao grew up to be a fine doctor. His clinic was called Sainath Clinic. It was at Worli, Mumbai.

Leela 75:   **Mahadev N.Chandorkar alias Bapu**

Bapu was blessed to be born to Baba's devoted Bhakta Nana and Radhabai Chandorkar in 1896. He was the younger of the two sons born in Kalyan, he was in close contact with Baba right from the childhood. In 1900, he was but four-years-old, when he applied *chandan* (sandalwood) paste to Baba's forehead, as he did to other gods he worshipped at home.

Till then only Mhalsapathy applied chandan to Baba's throat. Thus innocently he set the stage for ritual worship of Baba with all due formalities.

In 1908, he accompanied his father to Shirdi, he heard Baba say, "Tell Nana, he has been with me for so many years, yet he cannot understand that I am in every fly and ant."

This was said by Baba when he told Nana that he had already eaten the *prasad* in the form of the fly and ant. Bapu heard the words and they lodged in his heart. He learnt that Baba was Parabrahma and was indeed in every creature. He also realised that Baba had spoken the 'highest truth' that the Shastras teach. This truth he followed for the rest of his life.

Bapu (photo 38) did his primary education from Pune. He graduated from Krishna Karma Angle Vidhayala (College of Agriculture and Horticulture) with honours. Nana owned three hundred acres of land in Sonar Pada Gaon, 6 to 8 kilometers from Kalyan. Bapu tended to this and grew grapes and grains. He also had a dairy farm and milk and dairy products were sold to the neighbouring towns.

He married Girija Bai, the daughter of Trivikrama Kashinath alias Tatya Sahib Pithrae. He was an advocate from Dharar. Bapu states that time and again, Baba told him this – "Give alms, do good, Listen to your parents. Help your mother with her chores." But most emphatically Baba said, "Speak the truth and the truth alone." These words Bapu followed faithfully, throughout his life. Truth he knew was not the opposite of untruth, but a very comprehensive concept. It was all the virtues combined, like righteousness, integrity, humility, selflessness, sacrifice and surrender to Baba's will. Thus he helped the needy like his father. He donated the three hundred acres of land to make shelter for cows and cattle.

171

There was a raid by dacoits in 1942 and he lost a lot of his belongings. Following this he got sick and depressed. Dr Sardesai, a friend of his treated him. Dr Sardesai had an office in Telegaon and fields in Kamset. He advised Bapu to go to Kamset and recuperate there. Kamset was a serene, beautiful hill-station near Lonawala. So Bapu moved to Kamset. When he recovered he attended the fields.

After the tragic events in Maina Tai's life, Nana and his family went to Shirdi. Nana was upset and sat before Baba in sullen silence. Baba said, "Why are you so silent"? Nana dejectedly told him about the calamities that had befallen his family.

Baba replied, "The birth of a child, death of a relative are dependent on poorva karma. Even the great god who has created this world cannot alter these. Do you think he can tell the sun or the moon to rise two yards further from their usual or appointed place? No, he cannot and will not do that, that would produce disorder and chaos."

Bapu heard this and learned to acknowledge the wisdom of Baba's words. He had six children. All his children died except a daughter named Vatsala. He bore his grief stoically and with maturity. Vatsala got married and came to live with her in-laws in Pune. His daughter brought him to Pune in 1963 to live with her. He took samadhi in 1967 in Pune.

Leela 76: **Babu Chandorkar alias Vasudev Narayan Chandorkar**

Mention is made of his marriage in *Shri Sai Satcharita*, Chapter 46. He married Indira Bai, daughter of the daughter of Shrimant Jathar of Gwalior. Babu was Nana's eldest son. Unfortunately his date of birth is not known. He was born in Poona.

He studied there and graduated from Deccan College. He did his B.A in Mathematics, graduating with honours. During World War II he went on an assignment to Assam for two years as a civilian. He then worked as a teacher in Kalyan.

He often visited Shirdi with his father or with M. Pradhan. Once when he, along with his younger brother and M. Pradhan visited Shirdi, Baba was preparing handi for *Annadan*. Baba drove all the devotees out of the Dwarkamai. Much to his surprise Baba welcomed them. They stayed for a week, and Baba then gave them permission to leave. At that time Babu did Baba's 'Paad Puja' [Washing of His holy feet] and collected the 'teerth' and took it home to distribute to his friends and relatives. Thus he set the precedent for the ritual of 'Paad Puja'. After a very fruitful life he took Samadhi in 1958.

Leela 77: **Raghuvir B. Purandhare**

"I am connected with him for seven centuries. I will never forget him even if he is far away", said Baba to his mother on the very first visit to Shirdi in 1909.

Baba also asked him to build his very own house. Purandhare was rather poor as he was an orphan and earned twenty-five rupees per month. Besides he had a large family to take care of. "Do not take a single pie from anyone," said Baba. At first Purandhare dilly-dallied over it and whenever he met Baba, Baba asked him about the progress of the house. When he had no progress to report about, Baba abused him and threw stones at him for the delay. Dixit and Chandorkar offered to build the house for him, this enraged Baba even more. Purandhare then got a loan of five-hundred rupees from his office and brought a plot of land in Bandra. At that time it was a marshland and was deserted.

"I am here to look after you and your wife day and night," said Baba. It took three years for him to build and occupy the house. Now it is a multi-storeyed building and his grandson lives there (photo 45).

Datta Mandir, Dadar

Around 1909, Purandhare's wife had a severe attack of cholera. The diarrhoea and vomiting was relentless and the doctors gave up hope of her survival. He gave Baba's *udi* and *teerth* to her and went out of his home. He saw Baba standing at the side of this Datta mandir (photo 46). "Give her udi and teerth," He said and disappeared. He again gave her the udi and teerth and within half an hour she started getting better and recovered.

Baba's Silver Statue

Baba always took two rupees as dakshina from Purandhare. Curious about this, he asked Baba why the denomination '2'. "I do not care for the monetary value of the money", replied Baba. "But I want to stress *shradda* and *saburi*, so I asked of only '2'". Often times Baba gave Purandhare money that he carefully preserved in his place of worship and so did his son.

But what about the future generation? They may or may not know its value, so his grandson took all the silver coins (photo 48) to a goldsmith and got a silver statue of Baba (photo 47) made. He figured that the idol would be taken care off. This silver idol is worshipped daily.

Photograph of Baba

Baba gave many of his devotees money and photographs of Himself. To some He gave books and asked them to read, and meditate on them. He gave Purandhare his photograph (photo 89) who venerated it and prayed to it daily. Often times when he was in trouble he would sit in front of the photograph and cry his heart out and Baba would appear immediately and comfort him.

Leela 78:   Samadhi of K.J.Bhishma

In 1854, Krishna Shastri Jageeshwar Bhishma was born in Butti Bori, a small village near Nagpur. He was affluent, orthodox and totally involved in social services. Removing untouchability was his goal in life. His first wife died soon after marriage, so he remarried and had four children.

Then his second wife died. So he took sanyas. He renounced his wealth and property (he owned about ninety acres of land). He left his home and did *kirtans* and *bhajans* and wrote religious books. It was on the twenty-ninth of July 1934 that he took sanyas under the tutelage of Veda Maharishi Seetaram Hegdewar.

Before this he wandered about visiting holy places in India. Once he visited Amravati and met Dada Sahib Khaparde (photo 49) and they became friends. Dada Sahib brought him to Shirdi. (Mention is made in Khaparde's diary of his visit to Shirdi on 6th December 1911). At Shirdi the 'Urs' was celebrated on Ram Navami every year. In 1911, Bhishma was responsible for celebrating the birth of Rama or Ram Navami [*Shri Sai Satcharita*, Chapter 6].

Congregational worship of Baba started around 10th December 1909 with the onset of *Chawadi* procession. Bhishma was the author of *Sri Sainath Sagun Upasana* [aarti book] that was prepared and placed at Baba's feet around 1911. This is in response to Baba's asking him for five *laddoos*. Of the sixteen *aartis* specially written on Baba, the majority [that is nine], were composed by Bhishma. Bhishma spent the last years of his life in the Murlidhara Mandir at Mohappa (near Nagpur). He took samadhi (photo 40) on 8th August, 1935 after having attained tremendous spiritual powers.

Leela 79: **Lakshmi Bai Chinchnikar**

Lakshmi Bai's (photo 33) ancestors hailed from the small village of Khore, where she was born. Her surname was Purandhare. The Purandhares' were well off, they were farmers, and owned the farmlands. Lakshmi Bai was born around 1862. She was married to Anna [Damodar] in early childhood [child marriage].

Anna was about two years older to her. He was a 'Desasth Brahmin,' *Yajur Vedi* of the '*Athri Gothra*'. He was very affluent, and owned vast 'lands' in Vade, Nevale and Chinchni. Unfortunately there were legal problems with these lands.

Anna could neither read nor speak Sanskrit or English. Having spent most of his life in the small village of Chinchni. In fact, he had not travelled out of that village, nor visited any other city. Troubled by all these legal entanglements, and the constant fights with his relatives, he hoped to find peace and solace at the feet of a *satpurush*. Though not highly educated he had one good quality, and that was to document all his dealings, legally on paper. So, he gave the responsibility of the collection of the income, from the farms of Vade to Pandarinath Atamaram Babre [his relative]. He managed himself the income from Nevale and Chinchni. Though financially well off, he had no children. At that time the couple were in there fifties and had lost all the hope of ever having children.

His father passed away when Anna was a young lad. When he was about twenty years his mother passed away, and a few years later his younger brother also died. Thus Anna looked after and cared for his sister-in-law, who was issueless. Having settled all his finances, he was now free to go in search of his Sadguru. His utmost worry was "How to find an enlightened

Sadguru." But as they say, "When it's the right time the Sadguru, Himself finds you". As he was pondering about this he heard about the divinity of Sai Baba. Anna wasted no time, and set out with his family for Shirdi to have Baba's darshan. And the rest is history, a history that is evident even today. For the board above Baba's Chavdi reads 'Shri Sai Nath Babanchi Lakshmi Bai Damodar Babre, Chinchanakar Chavdi, Shake 1850' [See *Ambrosia in Shirdi* for details].

The couple made Shirdi their home and spent their time doing seva. When he came to Shirdi he stayed in Gondkar Gulley. Later he moved to Shinde Wada. Anna hardly left Baba's side. Baba called Anna by the name used by everyone and that was Anna. However, for some reason He called his wife "Haedambi" [Haedambi was a female demon during the *'Pandav* Dynasty']. Only Baba knows why He called this gentle lady Haedambi. Anna's favourite seva was to massage Baba's back, and stomach. This leela is described in *Shri Sai Satcharita*, chapter 24.

On 10th July, 1919 Anna made his will in which he gifted his property and estate to the Shirdi Sai Baba Sansthan. After all the legal ramifications and debts were paid off, the Sansthan was able to have a steady income of five hundred to seven hundred rupees a month. This money was used for Baba's naivedya and oil for lighting the *akhand* lamps in the Samadhi Mandir. This seva was very welcome in those days for the amount was by no means small.

This rustic, but great devotee breathed his last on 15th April, 1920. Lakshmi Bai died a year earlier. It was Anna's great desire to build a Baba Mandir on his property in Chinchni. His wish came to fruition and this beautiful Mandir stands on his property in Chinchni. The Shirdi Sai Baba Sansthan funded the building of this mandir   [Ref: *Sai Leela*, Ank 4, year 32, 1955].

Leela 80: **Abdul Jan Pathan**

Abdul Jan (photo 25) came to India from Tarbella when he was just a lad. He had a burning desire to go to Mecca, but had no one to support him. He landed at Manmad from where he was to go to Mumbai. On the way he heard about Baba's divinity, and how He liberally showered money on fakirs, and helped them to go to Mecca. So he came to Shirdi and he went to the Dwarkamai to meet Baba. He looked at Baba and Baba looked at him. Their eyes met, and Abdul felt the power. He at once felt that Baba was his Guru. Thus he stayed on at Shirdi. As a young lad Abdul was a zealous fanatic and regarded Hindus as enemies. But just after three years this view changed. He realised the futility of the animosity. The killings and destruction of religious places of worship saddened him. Baba worked on him mentally, and he never left Shirdi.

Baba asked him to stay at Kohrala a small village about twelve miles away. Abdul complied with Baba's wishes. He didn't go to Mecca, for he truly believed that Shirdi was Mecca and Medina. Just before he took Mahasamadhi Baba said, "Abdul ask for anything you want, and you will get it". Abdul replied, "Baba all I need is six feet of land to be buried in." His descendants still live in that house and his Samadhi is close by.

Leela 81:   **Ram Baba**

It was 22nd February, 1914 when Baba welcomed him saying, 'Ye kutte idhar aajana, Are! Jo hazam kar sakta wahi to kha sakta hai" [Roughly Translated – "You dog come here He alone should eat, who can digest it]. This leela is beautifully given in *Shri Sai Satcharita*, Chapter 23. When Chandorkar and Ram Baba came to the Masjid and found Baba eating *bhakari* with onions, Ram Baba was filled with doubt. He wondered how this person eating stale bhakari and onion help him.

Immediately Baba read his mind and said, "Nana only they should eat an onion if they can digest it." Hearing this Ram Baba (photo 67) was taken aback, and with a clear mind he asked Baba about his difficulty in attaining samadhi. Baba gave him the answers to all his doubts.

In 1910, Ram Baba took *sanyas* after having enjoyed life to its fullest. He was initiated into sanyas at Karanbas [District Bulandshahar] in Uttar Pradesh. Being of an ascetic nature he travelled widely and met many a Saint and spent time with them. He met saints like Ramana Maharishi and Swami Sivananda.

He roamed the jungles and mountains of India carrying his staff and a "Khapar" [begging bowl]. After meeting Baba his life changed forever. It was as if he had surrendered his ego at Baba's feet. In fact, he never used the word 'I'. In conversation he would refer to himself as Ram. He would address the devotees as "dear selves."

While doing "Parikrama" of the Narmada he met Hansdevji Maharaj, who sent him to meet Tembe Swami at Garudeshwar. Thence he went to Maninageshwar. It so happened that two

179

princes of Saurashtra came to Nathji Maharaj to take permission to go to Shirdi. Permission was granted and Nathji asked Ram Baba to accompany them. They made the journey by car and reached Shirdi just before the noon aarti.

Ram Baba went into the sanctorum and met Baba. Baba looked at him very intently. Their eyes met and the deep penetrating gaze, locked for some time about two minutes, and Ram Baba was never the same again. He felt bliss and ecstasy. He had received Baba's Grace.

Leela 82: **Bala Sahib Rudra**

In September 1905 Bala Sahib was born in Jalgaon [Khandesh District]. His father was a Superintendent of Police. In those days this post was highly respected, and paid handsomely. He had two paternal uncles, one was a lawyer and the other was a Sergeant.

The circumstance that brought his family to Baba was interesting. Once his grandmother Saraswati Bai and his aunt went on a pilgrimage to Gangapur. Bala Sahib (photo 78) who was ten-years-old at that time went with them. The pilgrimage was very fruitful, but on the way home, a strange incident changed their lives. As they were returning home they passed by a funeral pyre. A man was being cremated, when suddenly the corpse lifted his hand and held it high as if he was waving. His Aunt saw this and was stricken with fear. So scared was she that she started having loose bowel movements. Day in and day out she rushed to toilet. Many medicines were given to her, but the diarrhoea continued. Many incantations and religious rites were performed, but of no avail. Someone suggested that she should seek refuge in Shirdi.

That was in the year 1913, when Bala Sahib accompanied, by his grandmother and ailing aunt went to Shirdi. At Shirdi Baba applied *udi* to all of them, He gave his ailing aunt udi to be taken orally. After applying udi to Bala Sahib's forehead, Baba gently stroked his head, silently blessing him. Bala Sahib was intensely happy and his love and devotion increased.

Bala Sahib worked as an editor in various Marathi newspapers. He and his family settled in Pune. He lead a very spiritual life and was devoted to Baba. He died on *Gudi Paadva* of 2006.

Conclusion

In conclusion I would like to give some of my thoughts on 'Shiladhi'. To me Shirdi is the Mother. She looks after all her children whether bad or good. No matter where you are going in life all routes start from Shirdi.

Dr Keshev B.Gavankar writes, "That Adi Guru Shri Sankracharya from his locks gave the Ganga. Lord Shankar shook his 'Jaata' [*matted* locks] atop the Brahma Giri Mountain near Triambakeshwar, and outflowed the Godavari River. The meaning of Godavari is as follows. Go-Da-Vari. Go means Bhumi [Earth or land], Da means 'Giver' and Vari means 'Shrest' [best]. So Godavari means the land that gave its best or foremost.

The Ganga is revered in the north, and the Godavari is revered in the south. On the banks of this sacred river, many a saint sought refuge. And stayed there for long periods of time. Nivriti Nath met Ghaini Nath at Brahma Giri when he was doing *pradikshna* and asked him to spread 'The Nath Sampradaya' or the Bhakti Marg. Ghaini Nath in turn placed this task on the shoulders of Shri Dnyaneshwar. Thus the Nath Sampradaya spread far and wide, especially in Maharashtra. The people were steeped in the Bhakti Marg, numerous Abhangs, and bhajans were sung and the Warkari Sampradaya flourished.

Then the Britishers came and people sought a western life style. Slowly the bhakti marg was on a decline. At this critical juncture Baba manifested at Shiladhi. Shiladhi was then a small and remote village in Ahmad Nagar jilha, Taluka Rahata. It was situated about eight miles from the banks of the Godavari.

Shiladhi as it was called in those days was fortunate to have Baba walk on its soil and sanctify it. The word shiladhi can be broken into two root words – *shila* and *dhi*. Shila means mountain and *dhi* means *budhi*. So shiladhi means that '*gaon*' who's *budhi* is steady, calm, and serene as a mountain. So sacred was this village that saints like Ganga Gir and Devi Das came to stay there. As years went by, this shiladhi came to be known as Shirdi. Moreshwar Pradhan brought Shyam Rao Jayker to Shirdi. He wanted him to paint a portrait of Baba. In fact, he asked him to paint three portraits. So Jayker stayed in Shirdi for nine months. Every time he painted a portrait, Baba would tear it up, finally he painted the beautiful portrait that is now kept in the museum. Baba smiled and said, "Banao aur banao Mae tho gali gali maie rhne walla hun" [Make more and more portraits for I am going to stay in many a lane]. True to His word one can find temples of Baba even in the smallest or remotest lanes all over India.

Baba while conversing with Mhalsapathy would often tell him about the future of Shirdi. "Arre Bhagat this little village will become a famous place of pilgrimage. Huge palatial buildings will come up. Pilgrims will flock to this place from far and wide. Highly placed officials and famous people will visit Shirdi. There will be much pomp and show, Bhagat. In fact, people will be crawling like ants." To Shama and Tarkhad, Baba spoke of the future of Shirdi and said that "Golden Days are ahead of us." And so it came to pass, people from all over the world come to Shirdi. For once they come they have an irresistible urge to come again and again.